Shifting the Spiritual Atmosphere

Thirty Prayers ~ Thirty Days ~ Thirty Minutes

Part I
For the Individual

These prayers are designed to be prayed boldly, intensely and <u>out loud</u> in a declarative manner. As you pray, it is recommended that you personalize the prayers. Decree, also, all that the Father places on your heart as these prayers inspire you and precipitate others.

Prayer One:
Releasing Destiny and Favor of God

1. God, open the flood gates of Heaven over my church that I might advance in what You have for me during this season.
2. Break off fear, indecision and unbelief that would stop me from going forward and reaching my destiny.
3. I am a person of destiny; so is my church—individual and corporate destinies...destinies within destinies. Let them be released. I bind the enemy from stopping them and release freedom to be what You've called me to be and who You say that I am.
4. I release what You're saying over _____ (name your church)—not what others say! I say, "The church must line up with what God is saying. No more doubt and unbelief...no more shackles and chains...no more financial difficulties, no more lack."
5. I am breaking off lack and releasing Heaven's economy over my church family and me. Let the tithe come forth, in Jesus' name. Let the offerings come forth in Jesus' name.
6. Wickedness must go. I will walk in holiness. I declare, "Holiness today—HOLINESS over my family, my church and myself." Individual and corporate holiness, be released. Purity, purity, purity—that's my cry; that's my heart.
7. Let the 'favor of God' (FOG) come forth in all areas of my life...body, soul and spirit. I refuse to walk in the mundane any longer. I walk in the FOG all the time, taking ground from the enemy. *There is a way that seems right unto man but the way therein is death.* I walk in Your right way—the path You have for me.
8. I throw off plans, agendas, and ideas that are not from You and choose to align myself with You and Your Word. Let me be a student of the Word. How I long to walk in truth.
9. I only want to pray what's on Your heart, God. I want to hear what resounds in Heaven. I want heavenly visitations to come forth. I choose to know You intimately...a new level...a new height...a new depth...a new breath. What is it that You require of me? Of _____ (name your church)? Of my family? Of this body? Of this county? Release it, O God!

15

10. I pray for new waves of Your presence…from Heaven to earth—new shock waves that touch me and all that I'm about and all that _____ (name your church) is about. I invite You to break out and break into hearts and lives in a new way with a new anointing. I lay down what is in the way and stopping me. I tear down idols.

11. Birth revival through my prayers, supplications, and tears of mourning. "No more delay" is my cry. In Jesus' name I pray this. Amen.

What other prayers or thoughts has this evoked from you to the Lord? Write them here.

_____

_____

_____

_____

_____

_____

_____

Write personal notes, thoughts, and words you are hearing or sensing from the Lord. This may even include Scripture He is showing you.

_____

_____

_____

_____

_____

_____

_____

Prayer Two:
The Kingdom of God

1. I'm releasing myself, my family, and _____ (name your church) into Your plan once again—not for the good of myself but, more importantly, for the advancement of Your kingdom. Let Your kingdom come; let Your will be done through me...so that others may advance and reach their destinies. Help me not take my eyes off the prize—You! I seek You above all else. I'm *seeking first the kingdom of God and His righteousness and all these things shall be added unto me.*

2. As the kingdom advances, let many be saved—those whom You have ordained for the glory of God...those whose hearts will be pliable in Your hand...those who will become atmosphere shifters wherever they go...those who have been rejected and hurt by the world and Church but are not rejected by You. Let me and the Church not reject what You have accepted. Strengthen me for the task at hand. I say, "MORE, LORD, MORE!"

3. Let me walk in the NOW time, the NOW season of my life without looking back to what might have been. I leave Egypt to enter my promise land of what You have for me during this season. Let zeal and passion for what's on Your heart continue to guide me. I will have no regrets for what might have been, living my life to the fullest today! Make me part of a people group full of passion for the things of You! Let _____ (name your church) not waiver in devotion. Let me continue forward in extreme worship and praise that is full of passion for my King.

4. I declare, "Let the King of Glory come forth and let His presence overwhelm and overtake me." I want more of Your presence... more of You, Lord.

5. I release signs, wonders, and miracles, declaring You are the God of signs, wonders, and miracles. I decree, "You are God of the healing anointing. Sickness must flee; disease must go; health and healing are flowing at _____ (name your church). Heaven is open; angels ascend and descend for the glory of God." I invite You to "Come, Lord Jesus, come." I choose to make You famous above all else. I lay down my pride, for I know *You resist the proud but give grace to the humble.*

6. Let me take up Your mantel...Your mantel...Your mantel of

love. I choose to love with Your love. I choose to love with truth. I choose to love with compassion. Jesus looked and saw that *they were harassed and scattered.* Let me see what You see and may my heart be filled with compassion, O Lord. I release my heart to be compassionate and moved by what moves You. I refuse to walk in counterfeit compassion, which can take a form of ungodly or fake sympathy and even work out in flattery. I shun all counterfeits to walk in godliness toward my brothers and sisters, carrying the burden You have for them. I shake off the lies of the devil and yield my members to righteousness, leading to holiness for the glory of God and His Kingdom! I see the results. Unity is birthed.

7. I do what You say—not what I think. I choose to align my heart and mind with You and Your Word, not my opinion or the latest fad. Forgive me when I have placed these above Your desires, Lord. I repent for sins of omission and commission as I yield my heart, mind, and life to You. I turn myself over to You—body, soul, and spirit. I choose to worship You in spirit and in truth. Let it begin with me and my family. Let it transfer to the whole church…let _____ (name your church) become a praise in the earth as glory is brought to God and God alone! You are worthy to be praised! I pray all of this in the mighty name of Jesus, Amen and Amen.

What other prayers or thoughts has this evoked from you to the Lord? Write them here.

_____

_____

_____

_____

_____

_____

_____

Write personal notes, thoughts, and words you are hearing or sensing from the Lord. This may even include Scripture He is showing you.

_____

_____

_____

_____

_____

_____

_____

Prayer Three:
Normal Christianity:
Walking in the Supernatural

1. Let Your people come forth in these end times to reach the destiny You have for them. Let me go forward with Your anointing to heal the sick, raise the dead, and cleanse those with leprosy. Freely I have received, freely I give. Help me to walk in this with Your grace, character, and anointing.

2. Who can know the mind of God? I say I can, because Your spirit dwells richly in me. Because He calls me friend, I know the times and seasons I live in. I am instant in season and out with words of prophecy, words of wisdom, and words of knowledge at hand for those in need. I have all nine gifts of the Spirit at my disposal for use when needed. I do not shy away from being used, but go forward because I have exercised them, and You can trust me with them. *I do not give up in well-doing but in all my ways, I acknowledge You for You shall direct my paths.* I do these things for Your name's sake…that You might be glorified by my well-spent life. I say and declare **"You are worth it, Lord!"** How I love You! Help me to love You even more.

3. Jesus, Jesus, Jesus…how I delight in You, my God and King. How my heart beats to be in-sync with Yours. I am searching for ways to please You. Let this be the hour that I look and see, search and find, listen and hear what is pleasing to You above all else. Let me join with people who are so after Your heart that it causes the world to stop and take notice.

4. I say, "In the midst of the battle I will remain true to who I am, because You live in me. In the midst of what is taking place all around me, I take up my shield and buckler, and my battle cry remains consistent with 'who I am' in You." I don't back down; I advance, defeating the enemies of my soul and those things that would hold back what You are doing in me and in _____ (name your church). I say, **"No,** I will not back up or give in." I go forward in Your will and ways. I choose to look with spiritual eyes, not at what the world says I need to look at or be like. I refuse to be politically correct at the expense of being Biblically correct. I choose to be a person of the Word rather than one who bows at the altar of worldly opinion.

5. I choose righteousness, even when it is unpopular. I choose the way of love even in the face of adversity and lack. I declare, "You are God. You are more than able to help me even in trying and difficult times." Therefore, I choose to bless and not curse. I choose to believe the best. I speak life with my words, thoughts, and deeds.

6. I believe my prayers go forth and change the landscape of my circumstances, bringing Heaven to earth, allowing this age to intersect with that age. Therefore, I walk in the supernatural, believing that the supernatural is normal Christianity. Everywhere I go and everything I touch is changed because the living God lives in me. He and I make a majority and are able to change the unchangeable, think the unthinkable, and imagine the unimaginable for His glory and my good. I now live and think *outside the box.*

7. I crown Jesus king over my life. You are Lord of Lords and King of Kings. I declare this to the North, South, East, and West. **Who can deny this truth?** *Deep calls unto deep,* declaring "Jesus is Lord." _____ (name your church) corporately speaks the same. I take a stand declaring this day and night, night and day.

8. Sin must flee. Addictions of all sorts must go. I cancel assignments of alcohol, drugs, smoking, overeating, and sexual immorality. Pornography, lust, fornication, and adultery spirits must bow and let God's people go. Since none of us are immune from sin, sickness, diseases or curses, I release these prayers over myself, my family, and _____ (name your church).

9. I long to live in holiness, set free from the bondage of sin. I choose to forgive and have my prayers go forth uninhibited. I believe that You have come to set the captive free. *Those whom You set free are free indeed.* I claim this freedom for myself and those whom You have called to _____ (name your church). All of this is for the glory of God and in Jesus' name, Amen!

What other prayers or thoughts has this evoked from you to the Lord? Write them here.

_____

_____

_____

_____

_____

_____

Write personal notes, thoughts, and words you are hearing or sensing from the Lord. This may even include Scripture He is showing you.

_____

_____

_____

_____

_____

_____

_____

_____

Prayer Four:
One Nation Under God

1. I am part of a people group whose nation is God. I declare, "One nation under God—from sea to shining sea!" Let freedom ring in _____ (name your country) once again as I fall on my face and repent for the wickedness that I unwittingly have participated in, including the shed blood of the innocent and the atrocities against children and women in the name of sexual freedom. Forgive me, Lord, for my silence and lack of action. I stand in the gap and repent for_____ (name your country)—no longer believing the lies the enemy has perpetrated upon me. Help me to turn from my wicked ways. Come and heal our land. That is my cry; that is my plea. Do not turn Your face from me. I am desperate for You to come.

2. I shift my focus from the ways and wiles of the world to You. Give me eyes to see the hurting and lost. Send more laborers for the harvest fields. Use me, Lord. Help me get over my fear and go. Let me lead the charge. I have Your heart, Your words, and Your anointing. I am graced with Your presence in season and out to speak what's on Your heart. I refuse to allow fear—fear of man or any other source of fear—to grip me or stop me. I bind its power, in Jesus' name.

3. *You are the potter; I am the clay; mold me and shape* me for the Master's use. With Your strength flowing in me, *I will not grow weary in well-doing, but in all my ways I will acknowledge You. You will direct my paths*, for Your name's sake—not mine. I trust the same for my family and the corporate body at _____ (name your church). I charge myself and _____ (name your church) to line up with You that both might worship You with obedience. I choose Your way in all things…all things…all things Lord.

4. I stir up the gifts within me and call them forth. I exercise them and make myself available to You. Use me, O Lord. Take me to the next level. I stand ready as a *good soldier* in Heaven's army awaiting Your orders. Give me ears to hear and a willingness to obey 100 percent of the time.

5. I release _____ (name your church) to be a triple threat in this season. The church will walk in the triple threat

of prayer, prophecy, and praise. It will produce preaching that changes hearts and minds, while concurrently shifting the atmosphere and aligning the hearer Biblically with You. The result will be that *no good thing will You withhold from Your people*. I acknowledge that *God is on the throne and His Son is at His right hand interceding on my behalf*. Therefore, I have everything I need. I do not back down from the plans You have for me. The anointing is released over me day by day, hour by hour, and minute by minute. It is fresh oil, fresh wine, and fresh manna for all to taste and see that the Lord is good.

6. I proclaim that "God is good. He reigns; *every knee shall bow and every tongue confess that Jesus is Lord.*" I declare that to the highly organized powers and principalities that want to rule over my life, this county, and _____ (name your area); I tell them to depart because *Jesus is Lord* over me and this area. He is the commander of *all that __was__ and __is__ and __is to come__*. I yield to You and You alone. *Let all that has breath, praise the Lord.*

7. Let a holy hush fall on me that even the angels take note of what God is doing at _____ (name your church), in _____ (name Your county), in my family and my life. Let the trumpet sound and the Heavenly proclamation come forth that "**I have been set aside for the glory of God.**" Let Your praise ring aloud and many be touched, strengthened, and encouraged by lives that are sold out. Then may all give You glory, for *You alone are worthy.*

8. I see what my Father is doing and I do it. I hear what Abba—my Daddy–is saying and I say it. I align my heart and mind with Jesus also; Your infallible, undeniable presence fills me. It leads me and guides me in the path I should take.

9. I do not have to wonder what You're up to; I know by the sheer magnitude of Your presence in my life. I meditate on You and I am changed from the inside out. It is impossible to stay the same; You are directing my every thought and move. I am aware that You are with me, in me, on me, and around me at all times. What can be more excellent than that? How glorious are Your ways! How I live to taste the sweetness of Your presence! How I long for more! I say, *"**More Lord...more!**"* All of this is in the name of Jesus and for glory, honor, and praise to Abba Father Daddy. Amen.

What other prayers or thoughts has this evoked from you to the Lord? Write them here.

_____

_____

_____

_____

_____

_____

_____

Write personal notes, thoughts, and words you are hearing or sensing from the Lord. This may even include Scripture He is showing you.

_____

_____

_____

_____

_____

_____

_____

Prayer Five:
Prayer of Affections for my King

1. Let Your light so emanate in me, through me, and around me that all can see and know there is a God in Heaven who is madly in love with His children. Let me recognize the consuming fire of Your love that surrounds Your people. May I walk in such a presence that people are continuously drawn to me—which ultimately draws them to You. My goal is YOU and YOU alone. How I long for my heart to align with You in all areas. How I trust You to finish that which You've begun in me.

2. Let me walk in the salvation that You bought for me on the cross—the finished work...saved, healed, and delivered—100 percent of the time. Change my thinking to align with You and Your Word. May I know Your Word and trust You for the outcome.

3. *You are God and there is none like You.* I declare this for all to hear. I don't back down from my public displays of affection toward You, my Bridegroom. I lift holy hands to You. I kneel before You. I dance, sing, and shout in Your presence because I am so in love with You. My goal is that my affections will be toward You and You alone. I set my face like flint toward the *soon coming King*! How my heart palpitates at that thought.

4. So I declare, *"Open up ye gates and let the King of Glory in. Who is this King of Glory? The Lord mighty in battle.* You are my beloved *and You have stolen my heart."* You look at me and *though I'm dark, You say "I'm lovely."* How that brings delight to my heart and strength for this day and hour. I don't shrink back because my beloved beckons me to come. I hear You say *"Come up here. Come up here."* My heart races as I ascend to where You are. I am completely Yours for you alone are worthy.

5. I say, *"There is none like You."* I crown You King over my life and heart. _____ (name your church) delights to do this. The trumpet sounds and I hear You calling me. I tune my heart into Yours for *Your name's sake* and *the glory of God.* Let the Son be about the Father's business. I will look to see what You are doing and do it.

6. I invite the Holy Spirit to overwhelm me with <u>more</u>. I invite the Holy Spirit to teach me, lead me, and guide me in the way that I should go. Because of this, all I put my hands to prospers. I *cast*

my bread upon the water and watch it return to me. The heavenly interest comes forth and I operate in Heaven's economy, even in the midst of difficult times.

7. I also walk in health, grace, and freedom from the hands of the enemy. I am instant in season and out to be an extension of Jesus on the earth—*laying hands on the sick and seeing them recover; setting the captives free* with the message and prayer of deliverance; having the prophetic word to bless and encourage as the Lord leads me.

8. Because of this, my Abba Father Daddy receives glory from my life. I become a walking, talking extension of the Lord's grace in the earth today. Each test I encounter becomes a testimony— each mess in my life becomes a living message that advances the Kingdom of God. How that brings joy to my heart because I was created for this—to advance Your kingdom everywhere I go, with everyone I meet, and at all times. I surrender myself and _____ (name your church) to accomplish all that is on Your heart! Hear my cry, O Lord. Use me; accomplish Your goals with me at Your side—Your vessel of peace—Your instrument of righteousness, life, and love to a dying world in need of a Savior!

9. I say "Let that which You created me to be come forth. May the army of God arise in this hour and allow this to be the Church's finest hour." The enemy may try to overtake me and overwhelm me, but I stand firm in who You created me to be. I *stay under the shadow of Your wings and in the palm of Your hand.* I am protected and blessed everywhere I go because the living God is for me and not against me. He has made me *the head and not the tail.* I believe You for all good things and receive all good things because my faith is in step with YOU.

10. What can I say? *"Nothing can separate me from the love of God."* I say **"nothing"** because I have chosen to live this life for my King. Therefore, everywhere I go and everything I touch is *blessed. I am blessed coming in and blessed going out. The enemy is fleeing seven ways before me.* The things he has stolen from me are being returned to me sevenfold. I am walking in the number of seven—perfection and maturity. For I know that *when I see You I will be like You.* To God be all glory, honor, and praise forever and ever! I pray this for Your glory in the mighty name of Jesus. Amen!

What other prayers or thoughts has this evoked from you to the Lord? Write them here.

_____

_____

_____

_____

_____

_____

Write personal notes, thoughts, and words you are hearing or sensing from the Lord. This may even include Scripture He is showing you.

_____

_____

_____

_____

_____

_____

_____

_____

Prayer Six:
Breakthrough

1. Who knows what's on Your heart, O Lord? I declare, "I do, and so does YOUR church—the Bride who is *making herself ready.*" I stand in amazement at You, my Bridegroom and King. I declare, "I choose to make myself ready for You." I put on holiness, which takes me into Your chamber. I walk as a person separated unto You, for *You alone are worthy.* There is none like You.

2. The world stands and looks in amazement. When I clothe myself with You, I look different, act different, and sound different. The world senses the love of Jesus, yet cannot understand it until they come into right relationship with You. Therefore I proclaim, "Salvation after salvation, new babes come forth. Allow my words to be like *seeds that fall on good soil, producing crops that yield a hundred, sixty or thirty times what is sown.*"

3. Make me ready to receive them. You said, *"You lost none who were given to You."* May I have the same record? Show me how to raise Your kids, God. Teach me how to disciple them. For surely the harvest is coming. Prepare me for it NOW! Help me to know how to do what pleases You with every person—each individual treasure that You bring into the Kingdom. Show me how to set them on their road to destiny. Instruct me how to administrate what is on the Father's heart. I trust You for the final outcome that zero fall through the cracks and that my heart and goals align with Your Word *that none would perish but all come to the saving knowledge of Jesus.*

4. My heart cry is this: *"Jesus, Jesus, Jesus."* I proclaim that name to the North, South, East, and West. I take delight in that name. I stand together with the true Church as one voice to give glory, honor, and praise to Jesus. It is not only me, but my family and church. It is for all those who have been ordained for the glory of God. It is those whose names are written in the Lamb's book of Life. I hear You say *"come hither."* So I come. I lean into You. The breath of God touches me and I am changed.

5. How can I stay the same? It is not possible. Because I am changed, it changes my family and church. The corporate anointing for change brings forth the breaker anointing. God breaks into all my circumstances that I yield to almighty God. Every circumstance

bows to the power that is higher than sickness, disease, financial lack, rebellious kids, unloving spouses, marital unfaithfulness, fornication, pornography, drug and alcohol abuse, anger, rage, broken heart, depression, suicide, and poverty of the soul. These assignments of the enemy are cancelled—sent to the pit by the only name that has omnipotent authority to do so—Jesus Christ of Nazareth. I *reckon the old man dead and go forth in newness of life* for Your name's sake and the advancement of the Kingdom.

6. I say "Thy *Kingdom come; Thy will be done*." I decree, "Establish on earth what's in Heaven. *Thy will; not my will.* Your plans over _____ (name Your area)...Your voice—Your ways. *Make a way where there seems to be no way*." I take up my sword and shield...*putting on the full armor* to battle the forces in the Heavenly realm. It is my time to shine. It is also the Church's greatest hour. Let the people of God bow before their King. You reign and rule over all.

7. I don't *grow weary in well doing but in all my ways I acknowledge You* and consequently *my path is directed.* I understand also that *the heart of the king is in the hand of God.* Therefore I trust You to direct the king's heart in the path that it should go. Even when it is not the direction I think is correct, I choose to trust You Lord. I choose to bless and not curse. I choose to pray and believe the best.

8. You are the *King of Glory* and I long for Your coming. I long to see You. I long to know You. I long to be like You. My heart cries out for more of You, and the result is MORE. My capacity to hold You is expanded. I become less and You take preeminence in my body, spirit, and soul. I live for what's on Your heart. I am continually in contact with You. Your presence becomes more and more tangible day by day, minute by minute.

9. Since You have all the answers, I continually seek Your guidance. Things work out, because I'm working Your plan, not mine. Vain imaginations give way to kingdom realities. Therefore, I thank You for revelation upon revelation. I see clearly now. The fog is lifting; the veils are being removed; the scales fall away. Once again, I proclaim for all to hear..."How great is my God; You alone are worthy of all my praise and adoration!" Idols become non-existent. You are so huge in my life, my family's life, and _____ (name your church) life. Everything else pales

in light of my God and King! To Him be glory forever more, in the mighty name of Jesus, Amen!

What other prayers or thoughts has this evoked from you to the Lord? Write them here.

_____

_____

_____

_____

_____

_____

_____

Write personal notes, thoughts, and words you are hearing or sensing from the Lord. This may even include Scripture He is showing you.

_____

_____

_____

_____

_____

_____

_____

_____

Prayer Seven:
Unity

1. Lord, I take this time to declare that my delight is in You. Take me higher to that place where You and I can commune more intimately with more passion than I've ever known. Let _____ (name your church), my family, and me be people who are after one thing: YOU and YOU alone. My goal is that I might know You...that I would sense Your presence all the time...that my thoughts would be on You and that I would be about the Father's business...How I long to be with You.

2. John 17:3 states, *"Now this is eternal life, that they may know you, the only true God, and Jesus Christ, whom you have sent."* I partake of eternity and transcend this world to the supernatural realm now. As I do, allow me to be so heavenly minded that I am continually earthly good. I put into practice all that You have for me. I do not allow the enemy to steal from me any longer. The fruit of my labor comes forth in tangible ways and those around me take notice and give glory to You, my King and Lord.

3. I shout with delight, for my heart beats in sync with You. As this transpires, Your delight in me overwhelms every circumstance that comes my way. I become the victor, no longer a victim. My way of doing things changes, because I have the blueprint of Heaven for every situation at hand. I begin to walk in the higher ways, since all Your thoughts and ways are higher than mine. I transcend to that indescribable place of going higher and higher with You.

4. The King of Glory receives all praise for the unimaginable takes place and many are changed. All that choose You go from *glory to glory.* _____ (name your church) goes from *glory to glory.* Each family is aligned with the corporate glory that You have released. A new-found unity is there for me to walk in.

5. I declare, *"How good and how pleasant it is for brothers to walk in unity."* I live in a realm of thick anointing flowing down upon me as it flowed down from Mt. Herman to Mt. Zion. I establish a new power grid because I have stepped into that place where *nothing is impossible.* How can this happen? One word—**unity**. I declare it and release it.

6. I say, "As *much as it depends upon me, I will live at peace with others.* " _____ (name your church) lives in peace, and this releases corporate unity. It comes because I have <u>dethroned</u> myself and allowed the King of Glory to be <u>enthroned</u> upon my heart, leading the way because **"unity"** is His cry—even to the point that Jesus prayed that all would *be one even as the Father and He are one.* I press into it, receive it and my marriage flourishes because of it. I declare, "The enemy can no longer assault my marriage or those within my family and church." Jesus is crowned Lord of all marriages at _____ (name your church).

7. Anger is forbidden to raise its ugly head because that is not who I am. That spirit must flee, in the mighty name of Jesus. I will allow only righteous anger to overtake me. I declare, *"I know what is right to do and do it. "* I don't walk in deception, thinking that I'm doing what the Bible commands me when I've only read the Word and have not performed the Word. That type of deception must flee. I am *a doer of the Word;* therefore my life aligns with Scripture, and *things go well with me.*

8. I am *blessed coming in and blessed going out.* Your shadow, O God, falls upon me and the shadow of death flees from me. Life is released <u>over me, in me, through me,</u> and <u>about me.</u> Your shadow protects me as I lean into Your bosom and find warmth and comfort there. *The shadow of death* has no substance, for it is only a shadow and can hold no reality over Your people. I declare "*He builds a table for me in the presence of my enemies* and that is where I am seated to feast."

9. Not only am I kept by You, almighty God, and the angelic host, I am protected by the **breath of God**. I hear the wind of Heaven and know which way to turn. I allow Your Spirit to overwhelm me with love. You continually bless me with reassurance and release peace over me, my family, and my church.

10. Therefore I know Your plans. It is for the good of _____ (name your church), my family, and me. *You have plans for me to prosper.* You give me hope in every situation. Even when things go wrong, You are busy working all things together *for my good* because *I trust You and am called according to Your purposes.* This assurance goes with me wherever I go. I watch as You continually work this out in my life. Now, disappointment flees, and peace resides in me. My welfare is on Your heart and

mind. I trust You in all things, for *You are great and greatly to be praised! In Jesus' name I pray,* Amen.

What other prayers or thoughts has this evoked from you to the Lord? Write them here.

_____

_____

_____

_____

_____

_____

_____

Write personal notes, thoughts, and words you are hearing or sensing from the Lord. This may even include Scripture He is showing you.

_____

_____

_____

_____

_____

_____

_____

Prayer Eight:
Providential Blessing

1. Let Your light so shine before men that all would see You lifted up, praised and adored. I give You adoration, for You are due that. The enemy trembles and his minions flee when they see and hear the praises of Your people going forth; the true Church represents You on the earth as Priest, Prophet, and King. *"You alone are worthy to open the scroll,"* echoes for all to hear. I whisper, "There is none like Jesus. There is none who can compare to the Bridegroom."

2. You lavish me with Your love and thwart the attacks of my enemies. My relationship with my beloved is tangible and personable. It flourishes, along with my family and church. The declarations of victory come forth, and the *shout of the King* is in me. It cannot be contained or held back. It is like *fire within my bones* and must be expressed. This creates havoc in the enemy's camp and it cancels the 'no good things' he continually throws my way. How amazing this is! It cannot be seen, only discerned by the spirit.

3. So I cry out, "Sharpen my ability to discern. Give me eyes to see and ears to hear into the supernatural realm. Open my eyes as never before. Let my faith level rise and my thirst for truth overflow the banks of my being." I believe that in this time and this hour _____ (name your church) and its families are aligning with the Creator of the universe. The domino effect begins...thus aligning the churches in this county and all of _____ (name an area bigger than your immediate area). It goes forth to reach the state and nation. The riverbanks overflow; Your Word goes out in *power and might*. The gospel is preached; many are saved, healed and delivered. Healthy is my status and that of the people who continually 'walk-out' the confession that *Jesus is Lord* of their lives.

4. Though the enemy assaults me, I am a lover of the Word, being *instant in season and out* to pray at all times what is on the Father's heart. Because of this, my prayers are answered quickly. I walk in the realm that says, *"I've never seen the righteous forsaken nor His seed begging for bread."*

5. I know that I am anointed with the anointing that *breaks the yoke* and fills me at all times with all that God has for me. I have the ability and the capacity to reach up and pull down what the Lord has for me. I have learned to rid myself of earth-bound prayers—praying God's heart—heavenly prayers. These prayers capture Your attention, releasing the angelic host to perform all that's on my Daddy's heart. Once again, my prayers are releasing blessings that overflow to all who come in contact with me and my church. (SELAH)

6. Without a doubt, I declare, "No contest." You are the one for whom my heart longs; You are the one who leads me in the path of everlasting life. I say, "It's time for America to once again align with You." This is a country whose founding fathers' hearts were to worship You in all their ways. Even the buildings in Washington, D.C., shout glory to You. They magnify You with words of Scripture and adoration. They announce the providential blessing that flows out from the epicenter of our political structure. Even when sin abounds, Your grace abounds more as generational blessings continue forward and generational curses bow to the name of Jesus.

7. I continue to cry for mercy and holiness so that wickedness would not overtake the national blessings released by our forefathers. In spite of what seems like huge odds, I continue to seek You above all else. Though the tide of popular opinion is against me, I continue to pray, worship, prophesy, and press in. I don't back down or give up. For I know You are the One who holds this country in Your hands. I know that You are more than able to help me in my time of need. I say, "This is the time of need, Father. Show Yourself strong on behalf of _____(name your nation) once again. Let Your name be glorified from sea to shining sea. *Don't relent until all are fully Yours.*" In Jesus' mighty name I pray, Amen!

What other prayers or thoughts has this evoked from you to the Lord? Write them here.

———————————————————————

———————————————————————

———————————————————————

———————————————————————

———————————————————————

———————————————————————

———————————————————————

Write personal notes, thoughts, and words you are hearing or sensing from the Lord. This may even include Scripture He is showing you.

———————————————————————

———————————————————————

———————————————————————

———————————————————————

———————————————————————

———————————————————————

———————————————————————

Prayer Nine:
Watchman on the Wall

1. Let me rejoice and be glad in my God and King. You reign forever. You are high and lifted up; there is none like You. You are worthy of all honor, praise and adoration. Take my prayers and turn them into sweet-smelling incense to Your nostrils. Let them ascend on high to You, the Lover of my soul. I breathe in, and it is You; Your breath fills me to the fullest of my capacity. That's why I cry out, "Expand my capacity to hold more of You. Let me savor the sweetness of Your breath, and may Your presence so overwhelm me that I bask in the love of Your sonship." How is that possible? Only You know. Yet, I continue to long to be with You and experience You in this tangible way. Heavenly hosts adore You, and so do I.

2. The ways of the world dim in comparison to You—the joy of my life. The enemy sees this relationship and backs off. How can the enemy penetrate this love triangle? It is impossible; this love flows from the throne room of God through the finished work of the cross to me and back to its origination in Heaven. This cycle continues on and on. It provides a shield about me, my family, my church, and all whom I encounter. This triangle of love is from everlasting to everlasting.

3. I call out, "Stay near to me; don't allow me to walk a path that takes me away from You. Help me to realize when I'm doing this." My goal is to draw closer and closer. I want my love for You to surround everything that I say and do. Therefore my thoughts are on You. Everything filters through the YOU who indwells me. My spirit-man rises up and connects with the Holy Spirit. I am led into all truths as the Comforter teaches and guides me.

4. It is my good pleasure to stand in the gap for others...to be God's watchman on the wall...to be a defender of the weak in the courtroom of Heaven and to war against Your enemies. My delight is to see the captives set free. That is why I stay on the wall with eagle eyes, watching and praying...praying and watching. This will continue until I see You return in glory.

5. How I long to see salvation coming to the masses and the stronghold of the enemy brought to naught! I declare this nation was founded under God and I passionately declare, "Return to

those godly roots. Let the church wake up and plead with our Creator to rescue this nation once again. Let the churches open their doors and people rush to the altars, repenting and giving their hearts to Jesus." I release the churches to go to the streets and call the people to come to their Savior. I declare, "Now God; let it be now." I am hungry to see this nation turn back to You. I am thirsty for righteousness to be established once again. I look to You, my Commander and Chief. I follow You and You alone.

6. How I look forward to the day when the heavens part, the trumpet sounds, and the King of Glory is made manifest for all to see. Until then, I go about the Father's business with strength, power, and might from on high. I don't back off, and I refuse to be offended. I forgive every person who wrongs me or hurts me. I don't pretend that it doesn't hurt; yet, I have made a pronouncement to my beloved bridegroom that You are more important than my hurt, pain, and right to hold a grudge. This allows me freedom to be who God has made me to be. I no longer come into agreement with unforgiveness and drink its poison. I am totally free to walk in the way that holds destiny for my family, church, and me.

7. Who knows for what I was created except the Creator of the Universe? I will not say to the potter, *"Why have You created me* like this?" Instead, I will allow You to conform me to Your image and trust You that *the work You started in me will be completed.* This is also my prayer for my family and church. Therefore, I am more than assured that *when I see You, I will be like You.* There is no doubt that this promise is not for me alone, but for my family, church, and Your bride.

8. Joining with others, I go after the corporate anointing and find that yokes are easily broken. I stand in unity, releasing prayer covering and power that will bring the breakthrough. I am no longer standing idly by while the enemy beats up on my family and friends. I walk as *the head and not the tail.* I refuse to be the tail any longer. I was not created to be the tail. This is not pride, but a reality of who I am in Christ and also that is my inheritance because I belong to You.

9. This reality overshadows every other reality I have ever known or walked in. I am assured from on High that even when the shaking begins, I will be able to withstand it successfully,

for I have built *my house on the rock* and not on sand. My foundation is based on Scripture and not on some person or personality. I tear down those man-made idols and resist them at every turn. I look to see You and know that the King of Glory is on the way. Just one glance from You will hold me until then. In the mean time, I cry out, *"Open up ye gates and let the King of Glory in!"* This is what I live for; this is the longing of my heart. Take my prayers, Lord, and allow them to produce those things for which You have created me. I will *be about the Father's business* and I refuse *to grow weary in well doing* for I continue to learn how to rest in the midst of adversity. Even now Your presence overwhelms me in Jesus' holy and perfect name, Amen!

What other prayers or thoughts has this evoked from you to the Lord? Write them here.

_____

_____

_____

_____

_____

_____

_____

Write personal notes, thoughts, and words you are hearing or sensing from the Lord. This may even include Scripture He is showing you.

_____

_____

_____

_____

_____

_____

_____

Prayer Ten:
Islam Must Bow to Jesus

1. Lord, I continue to cry out, "More, O Lord, more." I command the spirit man within to be stirred up and to line up with MORE. My spirit connecting with Your spirit is what I'm longing for. Otherwise, dead works that cause me to step out of Heaven's realm come forth, and I operate in the flesh. I crucify my flesh because I want to be with You...in Your presence.

2. Holy Spirit, take me to that place where the longing of my heart intersects with Heaven and Your will is released over me. Corporately, _____ (name your church) walks in this heavenly intersection and brings the will of God to earth. The unction is for the corporate church and me, also. This produces overflow that floods this community as I help take it for Jesus.

3. I am forsaking the old ways—the way I've always done things. I position myself for all that You have for me. I long for just one glimpse of You...to feel Your presence. I'm like *the deer that pants for water* in a dry and thirsty land, longing to touch You. I go into that secret place where sin and lust can't exist, and there You are *in all Your goodness and majesty.* I long to see You with my eyes and experience You in this life—*in the land of the living.*

4. Declarations come forth from my lips that say, "**Now** is the time for You to be made famous throughout the entire earth. **Now** let the people groups all over the world hunger and thirst for You to show Yourself strong on their behalf...for Your name is to be glorified forever." I shout, sing, declare, and boast in You and You alone. When I do that, everything pales in light of the majesty of Your omniscient, omnipotent, omnipresent ways. The world bows before their King and shouts, *"Hosanna! Hosanna! Hosanna!"*

5. I say Islam must bow to the name of Jesus. I choose to love the Islamic people, as God does, for *God so loved the world,* but I refuse to prostitute myself with the spirits behind Islam. I choose not to come into alignment with its violence and abuse. Filled with righteous anger, I shout, "_____ (name your nation) will not be one nation under Allah. The spirits

behind this Islamic march on _____ (name your nation) must flee, in the name of Jesus. I forbid these spirits to plant themselves on this soil and in the hearts of our men, women, and children." I decree, "Let the praying church arise and overwhelm this power of darkness."

6. I stand and boldly declare "NO" to the Imams and clerics of Islam who have declared a holy jihad on all unbelievers or infidels. I bind up the murder and violence that goes along with this belief system. I break off the lie of the devil that this assures Muslims a place in Heaven. I join ranks with Christians everywhere who are taking a stand against this deception, praying that their eyes would be open and that *many would come to the saving knowledge of Christ.*

7. I am determined to vote out politicians who stand on the side of political correctness and tolerance at the expense of truth, justice, and righteousness. I agree with Scripture that says, *"Righteousness exalts a nation, but sin is a disgrace to any people."* My prayers go forth to stop sin in its tracks and will not allow this disgrace to be upon me any longer. I magnify the righteousness of Christ and come into agreement with all that His shed blood accomplished for humans everywhere.

8. I am a Christian who will not be easily persuaded, deceived, or lulled to sleep. The sleeping giant of the church awakens from its slumber and cries out, "**No more!**" My fellow believers and I draw a line in the sand and say, "It stops here. No further. You cannot have this nation! You won't infect my family or friends with Your rhetoric *of peace when there is no peace.*" I stand in the gap to repent for this nation from the highest level of government to the lowest for entertaining ungodliness in any form. I will not turn a blind-eye to the news media with their outright lies and deception. I trust the One who is faithful to stop it in its tracks. I release the angelic host to fight this battle alongside me. *My God reigns* will be the outcome of all this. To You be all glory, honor, and praise forever and ever! It's in Jesus' name that I release this, Amen.

What other prayers or thoughts has this evoked from you to the Lord? Write them here.

_____

_____

_____

_____

_____

_____

_____

_____

Write personal notes, thoughts, and words you are hearing or sensing from the Lord. This may even include Scripture He is showing you.

_____

_____

_____

_____

_____

_____

_____

Prayer Eleven:
Breaking Curses, Releasing Blessing

1. Let hearts, minds, and spirits in the people of this nation align for God's glory and good pleasure. I **now** come into agreement with the reason for my existence...to bring glory to my King... to know You, love You, and serve You forever. *Every knee will bow; every tongue will confess that Jesus is Lord.* My confession of faith makes darkness flee—light drives it away. All will know Your ways are majestic, O Lord. How awesome are Your thoughts toward me. How incredible that One such as You would even notice me!

2. *Your mercy endures forever.* Divine mercy is bestowed on believers and unbelievers alike, *for You show no favoritism.* (You *rain on the just and the unjust.)* I walk in this great mystery, and my heart beckons me to partake. Yet, if I'm not careful, this could be missed—looking for love in all the wrong places. The enemy of my soul and the one who comes to steal my destiny makes sure of this. He blinds me and slimes me with unexpected situations. Yet the One I was created for continues to bid me *come up higher.* Come up here.

3. The Word tells me (Isa 30:21), *"Whether you turn to the right or to the left, your ears will hear a voice behind you, saying, 'This is the way; walk in it.'"* So I listen and step out to do what You are telling me. My spirit soars as it comes into agreement with this. There is no other way to go but up...higher and higher... fuller and fuller...richer and richer in the knowledge and ways of God. I experience daily that which I had only read about or heard that others had walked in. Visions, trances, dreams, and prophesies—all of the supernatural—become my way of life. Walking on earth with my antennas in Heaven becomes the norm.

4. I declare *"I know what is right to do and do it."* Yet, I also know in the last days *wrong will be called right,* and *right will be called wrong.* I shout to the North, South, East, and West, **"What is wrong with right?"** The corporate Church takes its stand and does not bow to iniquity and perversity. I set my heart to hate evil with a perfect hatred and trust God to turn this nation back to righteousness. My trust is in YOU, my King, knowing that *You are more than able.*

5. I speak to mountains of poverty, spiritual lack, selfishness, unbelief, immorality, addiction, and pride. I command them to be cast into the sea. My mustard seed of faith is more than sufficient to accomplish this. I agree *as in touching* and see You, my Lord and Savior, set me free from any crisis at hand.

6. Those who are *weak become strong*, walking in *the power of Your might*—not the arm of flesh. This breaks off curses that come from trusting in the arm of the flesh. I have a new-found freedom that superimposes upon me things that *eye has not seen, nor ear heard, neither have entered into the heart of man what God has prepared for those that love Him.* How awesome is this! (SELAH)

7. I say I will not *let my heart be troubled; neither will I let it be afraid. I have chosen to put my trust in You* and You are unable to disappoint me. For I know *You reign* in all circumstances—past, present, and future. As I *plead the blood* that Jesus shed for me and walk in the finished work of the cross, I see and experience that *no weapon formed against me has legal right to prosper.* I have pulled the rug out from the enemy and stripped him of legal access to my life.

8. Because of this, I now see that the *words of my mouth and the meditations of my heart are pleasing to* God; what else can they be? I stand in the gap canceling every hex, vex, incantation, evil surmising, witchcraft prayer, and word curse ever spoken about my church, family, or me. I annihilate them in the name of Jesus and say, "They are null and void as if never spoken."

9. I meditate on Scripture and trust Him to *watch over His Word to perform what is on His heart concerning me.* Therefore I walk in generational blessing and prosperity of the body, soul, and spirit. Everything I touch is blessed; everywhere I walk is ground taken for the Kingdom. My belief system, based on the Word of God—the Holy Inspired Scriptures, is now my reality forever and ever in Jesus' holy name, Amen and Amen!

What other prayers or thoughts has this evoked from you to the Lord? Write them here.

_____

_____

_____

_____

_____

_____

Write personal notes, thoughts, and words you are hearing or sensing from the Lord. This may even include Scripture He is showing you.

_____

_____

_____

_____

_____

_____

_____

Prayer Twelve:
That We Might Know You

1. Hearken! Alas! You draw near to Your children. Your right hand of blessing reaches forth and so does Your left hand of judgment... Blessings overtake those who do Your will and accomplish Your bidding. The left hand is there for those who refuse this. Yet the cry of my heart continues to be "mercy, mercy, mercy!" What else am I to say except "mercy"? For *Your mercy is new every morning* and it endures forever. Generational blessings go forth for a thousand generations to those who obey You and uphold Your commands.

2. The light of Your love shines forth into the darkness, and it flees. The generations advance in blessing because of the overwhelming love of Your virtue that adorns them. My family and I take refuge in You. My delight to do Your will remains my highest priority. *The Lamb of God who takes away my sin* releases all that I need for every situation. I sit with You and find the greatest contentment of my heart. All longings, desires, and wants are fulfilled in You. (SELAH)

3. I don't let mere facts get in the way of truth and reality. As I enter into that higher reality, I ignore facts on my quest for truth. Your ways are true. Your thoughts remain at the front of all I do and say. This stuns me and I awaken to the change that brings delight to Your heart. I adorn myself with the pleasures that come from holy and righteous living. I proudly wear You like a mantel for all to see.

4. Because I am still *in the world, but not of the world,* as I am interacting with those around me, the result is they receive a touch from You just by being near me. (I can barely grasp this mystery.) How great are Your ways! I can only imagine things so wonderful; yet, my heart yearns for this like a nursing baby longs for its mother's milk.

5. That I might know You! That is the cry of my heart, O Heavenly Daddy! That I might know You and walk in Your ways...that Your presence fills me and overwhelms me. I sit beside You and ponder, "Is it possible to be with You in Your presence and not be changed? NO! Is it possible to enter into that unknown realm and remain the same? NO!" This thought overtakes me and possibilities become reality. Even my DNA changes for good.

6. My plea is simple: "Continue to reveal Yourself to me. Bring forth the revelations of Your heart. Release it for this dying generation that has departed from Your ways and refuses to consider Your thoughts." Oh, Lord, how can one so awesome and majestic be ignored? Since this possibility advances toward reality, I pray, "Never, Lord, never."

7. How do I communicate You to unbelievers, atheists, agnostics, and pagans? Give me words that penetrate to the heart so that none can resist You. Let my connection with You be so strong, yet so sweet, that Your words are always on the tip of my tongue ready to be spoken—like *apples of gold in settings of silver.* My thoughts replaced by Yours—Heavenly thoughts that transcend this world to produce words that yield kingdom decisions on behalf of the unsaved.

8. My loud cry penetrates the atmosphere, "Stir things up. Turn this world upside down for Jesus. Tear down the kingdom of darkness. Reveal the Bride of Christ. Advance the Kingdom of God! Charge!" Don't stop until *Your Kingdom comes; Your will is done on earth as it is in Heaven.*

9. Break up the fallow ground of the hearts of Your people. Cause me to be pliable before You. Take me at my word and release the secret weapon of warfare—love that produces forgiveness and brings repentance. I commit to stand in the gap and make up the hedge for hundreds, thousands, tens of thousands and more. I know that *one can put a thousand to flight and two, ten thousand.* How is this possible? Yet, I believe for it. Once again I yield to the upside down Kingdom that holds life everlasting for all and remains a mystery. Let God be praised forever, in Jesus' name, Amen!

What other prayers or thoughts has this evoked from you to the Lord? Write them here.

_____

_____

_____

_____

_____

_____

_____

_____

Write personal notes, thoughts, and words you are hearing or sensing from the Lord. This may even include Scripture He is showing you.

_____

_____

_____

_____

_____

_____

_____

Prayer Thirteen:
Awaken Church!

1. How can I reach the heights of Heaven where You rule and reign? How do I get to where You are? Take me there. That is my heart's cry. I look to see You; I seek to find You; I reserve this time just for You. No other focus, no other interruption—just You and me. Let that heavenly presence melt over me. I soak and bask in You and You alone. I don't give up, for I know that when *I seek You, I will find You.* I hear, *"Be still and know that I Am God."*

2. So in the quiet, my heart waits and rejoices in the pleasure of You—my King. The delight that I draw is strength to my being and life-giving breath. Without it I would suffocate. As I lay in Your arms, soaking up the love of my Bridegroom, I hear the beat of Your heart for Your people around the world.

3. It brings me back to reality as I sense Your sadness and love for the lost, hurt, dying, and oppressed. This strengthens me for the battle at hand. The intensity of the moment explodes with purpose. For this I was born…to enter into the fight for all that really matters—the Kingdom of God, eternity, bringing Heaven to earth, and aligning myself, my family, my church, this area, and this nation with Your purpose and plan.

4. So again, I cry out, "Awaken, church, awaken!" to the God of the universe…to His purposes and plans. How much time must pass before your eyes are focused on what God focuses on?" Now is the time, Lord; allow me to see You in Your glory. Let me go about the business of seeing many saved and made disciples of the Most High God.

5. Help me see the church emerge once again with Holy Spirit convictions, not swayed *by every wind of doctrine, but able to rightly divide the word of God.* Then and only then will the world arise and take notice. They will exclaim, **"Surely God is in this place."** An explosion from on high will target and regenerate hearts and minds, advancing the kingdom of God one person, one soul at a time. How my heart longs for this.

6. If You would tarry too long, all would seem lost. But I know You are God and You hold time in Your hands. I praise You that things happen in Your time, in Your way, and *for Your good pleasure.* Every trial and tribulation bows to You, my King. Without a doubt, all things bow to You—even the systems of the world.

7. Every political official and judge, from the highest to the lowest, is responsible and answers to You. Babylon, the great harlot; the world's financial institutions must bow to Jesus. Thank You for holding it all in Your hands. Many are counting the cost of what their lives have amounted to, as some have *built their house on sand* instead of the rock. They now realize that the result has been that *all is vanity.*

8. I cry for "accountability and blessings. Stinginess, selfishness, pride, self-importance, envy, self-reliance and jealousy must go." In its place I declare, "godliness, freedom, holiness, generosity, humility, hard-work, perseverance, and fortitude." The church arises to take back what is rightfully hers. In the midst of suffering and lack, it is her finest hour.

9. The people of God arise and receive *the mammon from the wicked that has been stored up for the righteous.* You, the King of the Ages, prove Yourself faithful once again as I call upon You in my time of need and desperation. You hear and answer. This echoes throughout the whole earth as people are drawn to You. The Word tells me that *when You are lifted up* (in good or bad times), *You draw all men unto Yourself. That sounds like change to me—real, anointed, and unadulterated change that takes place in the heart and connects with the mind; bringing forth body, mind, and spirit that align with the King of Glory.* Release this plus more O Lord, in Jesus' mighty name I pray, Amen!

What other prayers or thoughts has this evoked from you to the Lord? Write them here.

_____

_____

_____

_____

_____

_____

_____

Write personal notes, thoughts, and words you are hearing or sensing from the Lord. This may even include Scripture He is showing you.

_____

_____

_____

_____

_____

_____

Prayer Fourteen:
Strengthening Marriage to
Break-Free from Divorce

1. It is never too late to release the greatness of God over the situations at hand. Lord, You *never tire or sleep.* Because of Your omnipotent nature, I trust You with all things. Nothing is too difficult for You—absolutely nothing. That's why strangers adore You. I wrap myself around You and choose not to let go. I know the ride ahead is more marvelous because I'm intentional in the things I do—choosing to place You in the center of everything. Your ways overwhelm me and become a fragrance that becons me to You. I am not silenced by the nay-sayers, because You have my rapt attention.

2. I take a stand, praying fervently, "Forgive America for its lax stance on pornography, the sexual slave trade, and abortion." Just because I haven't seen it taking place doesn't mean You don't. Just because I don't feel the pain first-hand doesn't mean You don't. "Break my heart with what breaks Yours, Lord. Remove the walls, the scales, and the hard crust from my heart that blocks me from this."

3. Lord, *against You and You alone have I sinned.* Constantly I observe sin that plays out in lack of love and commitment to the marriage covenant. This causes divorce rates to soar and children to suffer without both of their parents in the home. The hurt and pain is then put on display for the world to see as case after case goes before a judge and the judicial system intervenes with orders that may or may not release Your will for each family. This tragedy must be abated!

4. Stop it in its tracks and turn the hearts of Your people back to their spouses. I release devotion over marriages—my marriage (or future marriage). Give me a heart that has passion for the one with whom I made (or will make) a covenant. Let me not lose sight of Your plan for my life and how it interconnects with my spouse (or future spouse). I bless my spouse (or future spouse) with every good thing. I declare, "Faithfulness, love, and the ability to go the extra mile." I make a demand on the anointing for not only my marriage, but all marriages. "Release more grace," I pray. I remain unsatisfied until You invade Your

presence into every aspect of my life, marriage, and family. I declare victory over the enemy, commanding him to **"back-off."** I release *angels* to minister to the areas where I fall short. "Help me, Lord!" That is my cry.

5. Lord, Your Word tells me that You *hate divorce*; I understand why. Your children are overwrought with suffering resulting from the anger, rage, hurt, rejection, and pain of this stench. What does this broken covenant teach the children? What message are they receiving? How does this play out in their lives? Could it be that this results in addictions, mental and physical illness of all kinds, rebellion, depression, and sexual immorality? Where are the stalwarts who will cry out for these hurting, broken people? Who will even notice?

6. My cry today is "Help! O Lord; forgive this nation and its people for willing and unrighteous participation in divorce. *Make a way where there seems to be no way;* break off this generational curse. Rise up and defend the defenseless; rise up and empower those who are downtrodden under this adversity and travesty. Provide judges who will make righteous decrees in the face of this. Empower them with grace from on high to go against the tide of popular opinion so that Your people can remain afloat and their children can persevere when all is against them and their lives are crashing in. Help in this dark hour, Lord; my cry is for help!"

7. Lord, I pray for those who have innocently participated in divorce—not knowing any better...or prior to their salvation. Lord, remove the scars, guilt, and shame that so many continue to carry as the enemy reminds them of their past. Help them receive the love and mercy that God freely gives them as children of the Most High. I release the fragrant incense from the throne that reminds me *there is no condemnation in Christ Jesus.*

8. Forgive this nation for allowing drug addiction, alcohol abuse and addictions of all sorts to become rampant and the grief that accompanies this—especially since it often begins at a very young age. What is this teaching children and this generation? It tears apart families bringing guilt, shame and destruction. It even robs kids of their youth and continues to steal from them in middle age only to bring horrific and untimely death. If death does not come prematurely, the suffering continues like clock-work into old age, leaving people ravished in every area of their lives—without health, the love of family members or friends,

and penniless. This is the work of the one who has come *to rob, kill, and destroy.* Use these words to halt this, I pray!

9. Television shows and movies depict this with frivolity and light-heartedness—trivializing its sinfulness and its outcome. Teenagers become hardened to this and believe it to be normal. Forgive! Lord! This is **NOT** who You created me to be! That cry swells from the depth of Your being to me...the intercessor within screams for "justice and relief. Where are the people of God with righteous indignation?" Bring me back to the basics.

10. Therefore, my cry is for help and intervention. The orphaned generation that falls prey to this is pitied, but left to find their way all alone; few bother to care, most pretend not to notice. Yet, I know that You love them and feel their hurt and pain, even though they may no longer be a functioning part of society and so conveniently take their places in the ranks of one more victim of Satan and his demons. Lord, teach me to pray for this hurting group of people. Show me how to love them not only with my prayers, but also with my actions...in Jesus' consuming and compassionate name, Amen.

What other prayers or thoughts has this evoked from you to the Lord? Write them here.

_____

_____

_____

_____

_____

_____

_____

Write personal notes, thoughts, and words you are hearing or sensing from the Lord. This may even include Scripture He is showing you.

_____

_____

_____

_____

_____

_____

_____

Prayer Fifteen:
Prodigals, Burnt Stones, the Forgotten, and the Hidden

NOTE: The term *burnt stones* mentioned in the first paragraph below was coined by someone in a prayer meeting I attended. It speaks of people who have been hurt or burned out by the Church. It can also refer to wounded warriors—those with battle scars received in the spiritual line of fire.

1. Lord, I'm praying for people who have lost their way—prodigals, burnt stones, the forgotten, and the hidden. I sense their pain and look to see who will cry out for them. Who will call their name before the throne of grace? In this place of desperation, who will stand in the gap between the porch and the altar shedding tears for them? Here I am, Lord; use me. Allow my prayers to echo in the heavenly chamber and court room.

2. I say, "It is time for them to grab hold of their destinies, for the enemy to stop harassing them, and for their spirit-man within to rise up." Hold on for the ride; the King of Glory comes to the rescue. Don't relent until the hidden and hurting ones are again fully Yours, Lord. Take away that which hinders. Open eyes to the higher reality—Your will and Your ways.

3. I see the dungeons in which circumstances and bad decisions have placed people. I understand the pit that's been dug. "Is it possible to escape?" is their cry. You hold the answer; You hold the key. If this is not the situation, show what is taking place. If You are holding them captive for Your greater purposes, make it evident to each. So today, I set aside this time and allow the key of prayer to echo forth that You would have mercy, cancel the assignments of the evil one, and send the angelic host to defend the hurting, hopeless ones.

4. His forces seem to be laxly arrayed, for there has been little warfare on their behalf. Seemingly with ease, he has held the captives in captivity, lulling many to sleep; most have lost their desire to fight any longer. So, I call out, "Awaken! Align once again with the Kingdom of God. Allow God's army of angels to come and rescue. Do not align any longer with luke-warmness

and life patterns that hold many in status quo." Today I declare, "Break-through and break-out."

5. Release the Esther, Joseph and Joshua generation to receive divine revelation to their calling. Help me understand my anointing *for such a time as this.* I set aside time to release prayers that echo throughout Your throne room that You would have mercy and send Heaven's angels to minister to the prodigals and hidden ones. Bring divine revelation. Cancel assignments the evil one has lobbied against this entire group of Your hurting children. Release this Papa Daddy/Abba Father, I pray.

6. *God, You are not a man that You should lie.* You have come to set the captives free. So, I release a prayer of breakthrough that allows breakout of Your prodigals and burnt stones. Remove their hurt, O Lord; remove their pain. Let the injustices be accounted for and the court room of Heaven convened for the taking back of what the enemy has stolen. Today is the day of receiving seven times what has been taken. I say, "Let it be today…for their good and Your glory." I fight in the heavenly realms, tearing down strongholds, appropriating what and who they are in Christ…no longer held captive by the enemy. I understand that You not only promise, but You also deliver!

7. I hear the cries of the hurting, "But God, I've done all I know to do. What else am I to do? *If You but say the word, Your servant would be healed.* I can only do what I know to do. Teach me, O Lord; help me. I'm desperate. **Do You hear me**? **Where is the answer**? I have set my face as flint. *Though You slay me, yet will I serve You. I will not grow weary in well-doing. I'm choosing to acknowledge You in all my ways.* Please hear my cry. *Direct my path* and it shall be directed. I give You permission. Do whatever it takes that I might hear You. My only desire is to obey You. How I long for You; how I thirst for You in this dry land. When will this end?"

8. Lord, teach me how to minister to these, the hurting. Send more to minister. More ministers are needed. Turn all that love You into walking, talking ministers of the gospel of Jesus Christ. Show me how to walk in the fullness of the cross, giving away the total package—saved, healed, and delivered. Give me the right words to say—words that will reach into the depth of their beings to release Your kindness and love for them.

9. I choose Your ways in this land that reeks desolation for many. In the midst of this, I continue to believe that *I am more than a conqueror in You and Your grace is sufficient for me. Nothing can separate me from You...not death nor life... not angels nor powers or principalities...not things in the present nor things to come...*not even divorce, addictions, hurt or pain. Thank You for Your great abounding love that won't allow me to be separated from You. What does that look like? What does it sound like? What does it feel like? I yield myself to You and say, "Let it come forth, guiding my life at all times so that my path continues to be straight— *walking the narrow path...running the race* You have *set before me.* All that I am or ever hope to be, I yield to You. I am Your vessel, O Lord. I am Yours...I am Yours...I am Yours...I beseech You, O Lord, in Jesus' name, Amen.

What other prayers or thoughts has this evoked from you to the Lord? Write them here.

_____

_____

_____

_____

_____

_____

_____

Write personal notes, thoughts, and words you are hearing or sensing from the Lord. This may even include Scripture He is showing you.

_____

_____

_____

_____

_____

_____

_____

Prayer Sixteen:
A Prayer of Worship, Adoration,
and Obedience

1. "Awake! Awake! O sleeper...for the time has come and now is for true worshippers to worship God in *spirit and in truth*." It is time for You to receive the worship and adoration I long to give You and that You deserve. You call out to the worshippers, "Come." Do I hear You calling? Does my heart alight with Your presence when You call to me? Yes, it does...for I long to love on You.

2. Help me, Lord! I don't know how to do this. Teach me; show me; equip me so that the longing within can be satisfied. I am a vehicle and a conduit of worship. I release this for myself, my family, my church, this county, state, and nation. Teach me how to love on You through worship. Begin with me. I release myself today. Grow me up in true worship, Lord. Because of Your *great mercy,* I freely choose to *offer my body as a living sacrifice—my spiritual act of worship* to You—*my reasonable service. I'm choosing to be transformed by the renewing of my mind and to no longer be conformed to this world. Then, I will be able to know Your will...Your good and perfect will.* I choose to do this as a child of the most High King. I declare that I am a worshipper, and that is what I will spend my life doing and being. All that I know that I am, I lay at Your feet. I put on the mantel of worshipping my King, for You alone are worthy to receive all the worship I have within me.

3. Lord, help me to let go of all the ways I concocted to please You, but were neither in Your heart nor how You wanted to be worshipped during this time and season. I take off the old wine skin of worship and put on the new. I choose to love You with Heaven's love language and present myself to You in ways that please You. I adorn myself with what is pleasing in Your sight. I demand that my spirit-man within wake up and fully participate anew! I speak to my soul and flesh and forbid it to interfere with this undertaking.

4. I bow before You. I shout, sing, cry, dance, march, stand, yield to You and You alone. Whatever pleases You, King Jesus, is what pleases me. I wave my flags before You; I paint my pictures;

I sing prophetically—Heaven's songs; *I shout with the voice of triumph.* I even sing songs that may not be my genre, but are Yours. This releases the fragrance of Your presence that overwhelms me. The delight of You surpasses human understanding and words become inadequate to express what's within Your love-sick child who only have eyes for the beloved bridegroom.

5. If it were possible, I would write it in the sky for all to see and know. If it brought You more delight, I would shout it from the housetops. My declaration of being a true worshipper begins with just a heart whisper, going into prayers spoken aloud, then to a low roar, turning into a tumultuous, uproarious sound that culminates in oblation to my King...*Emmanuel—God with us—*the shout of my heart...the cry from within.

6. Let all who know my King cherish and obey You with obedience that is demonstrated in worship. Could it be that obedience is actually the highest form of worship? That is something I need to ponder. This one thought compels me to set my face like flint: that I might worship You more and more each day, each hour, each moment I obey. Let the world be a witness to obedience that is radical, yet fills the longings of Your heart.

7. I move into dancing before You. I enter Your chamber to dance at Your feet. I grow weary in many ways, but this is not one of them. You deserve all the praise I can bring. You deserve all my adoration, for You are King of Kings and Lord of Lords. *What more can I give?* is my question. How can I model worship that causes even the angels to stop and take notice? I'm not at that place yet. Once again I cry out "Help! Will You teach me? Will You show me? I am Your student!"

8. I long to present myself as a *living sacrifice* because *that is my reasonable service.* Listen, to my cry: "Take me deeper...take me deeper in this thing called worship." Let me crown You with the loving kindness that You not only deserve, but my heart overflows with to give You. Then and only then will I begin to experience the *height, depth, and width of Your love* toward me. How awesome this will be. How I linger just a little longer...one more moment...one more touch—that's what I want...just to be with You.

9. I do whatever it takes to be with my Jesus...divine connection is what I desire. Could it be that Your longing to be with me is even greater than mine? Now, I know that I know...I am a

supernatural being locked temporarily in this natural body, not the opposite. What could be more wonderful than an encounter with the One for whom my heart longs—brought on by the worship that You deserve? I now see Heaven coming to earth and earthly vessels encountering Heaven. All I can do is bow—breathing in and breathing out Your presence—with a heart that exudes thankfulness over and over and over again. All of this is for Your glory and in Jesus' name, Amen.

What other prayers or thoughts has this evoked from you to the Lord? Write them here.

_____

_____

_____

_____

_____

_____

_____

_____

Write personal notes, thoughts, and words you are hearing or sensing from the Lord. This may even include Scripture He is showing you.

_____

_____

_____

_____

_____

_____

_____

Prayer Seventeen:
Calling Forth All Singers, Musicians, Worshippers, and Intercessors

1. "It's time, Lord! Open my eyes; move me beyond my little caveat in my little world to Your possibilities…to Your potential. Release the hidden potential into reality. I say it is time for the musicians, singers, and intercessors to arise!" I trust You for Heavenly orchestration that plays out in day and night prayer. I am calling to those who have been called, disciplined, discipled, and destined to come before the King in worship and prayer. You said, *"my house shall be called a house of prayer."* Therefore I declare, **"Fill the Church; fill _____ (name Your church) with intercessors, Lord!"**

2. I call to the North, South, East, and West, "Intercessors and worshippers, come forth. That for which you were created is beckoning you." Do you feel it as you come and go? Do you sense it in the night watch? Do you see the fit? It's like a hand in a glove—exactly for what you were created. I declare, "Now is the time to say yes to your heavenly Daddy. Now is the time to allow yourself to submit to the promotion to which God calls you."

3. *Promotion comes from the Lord.* You are making your desires known to me. I hear You. The sounding of the call is loud. Heaven shouts, **"It's time! It's time! It's time! Release the singers; release the musicians; release the worshippers; release the intercessors**…all to their call…to their duty stations. Let the priests come forth; let the tribe of Judah arise in this hour to lead the people of God." That is Heaven's declaration. *Let those who have ears to hear, hear what the spirit of God is saying.* Let them take their stand to participate in their life calling and destiny.

4. I come into agreement with this, bringing Heaven to earth… bringing the supernatural into the natural realm. I do this today with my prayers and declarations. How can I do anything but come into agreement with You, my King? What is stopping me? Who is stopping me? In the mighty name of Jesus, I say "NO!—to every *power and principality in high places that have arrayed themselves against me!"* I contend with these evil forces and shout with all my might, "You will not stop God's people! I

release Your plans and purposes to come forth. I forbid anything less than Your perfect will and destiny to transpire."

5. My prayer for this takes the form of a war cry from the warrior within. The angels are released and begin to set things in order. I don't hold back; I won't relent until the release has come full circle and the worshipping intercessors step up to the plate to pray and do what is in the heart of the Father for this generation. "Where can I go that You are not there? How can I escape You?" Even though that is my first thought, I know it was for this that I was created; therefore I forget trying to escape. Instead, I yield myself willingly to the call upon me for prayer and worship.

6. "But, I don't have time" is the whisper under my breath and also from those that feel the tugging and know the mandate. The spirit answers back, "Yes you do! Yes you do!" So, I pray wherever I am and whenever I can to fulfill this mandate—driving the car, cooking, cleaning, and working. I now understand it's everywhere...all the time! This is not only my lifestyle, but the lifestyle of the Bride—the Church.

7. So, I release prayers today that "many will begin anew, picking up this call, including those who have let go of this desire for whatever reason, and especially ones who have been set apart *since before creation* for this." I declare, "**Let the *set apart ones* come forth. *Stop kicking against the goads.* Get in God's** presence, <u>pray</u> His will, <u>sing</u> His song, <u>release</u> deliverance over His people—over the world." I say, "Align yourself with God for it is a NOW time and a NOW season."

8. Who can flee Your presence? Wherever I go, You are there. I cannot resist that for which I was created! Only I can make that choice for me. But, I say to all, "<u>Listen</u>...for the Father is calling; <u>listen</u>... for the time of release is now; <u>listen</u>... for I know You are establishing Your will on the earth." Today, I'm praying and releasing the ability to hear clearly. The word I'm releasing is **clarity**. Let clarity come forth for the people of God.

9. The question, "Who will participate? Who will involve themselves with the *bread of life* and the *light of the world?* Who will be bread or light to another?" It is as simple as "yes" <u>or</u> "*make me willing to be willing.*" I release strength, power, and might over those who are hedging <u>and</u> over those who have said "Yes." My cry is, "God, use all the worshipping warriors and intercessors for Your good will and pleasure."

10. Release Heaven's perfect will to come to earth through prayers, songs, and declarations. Take me to the next level. Teach me supernaturally. Let me progress beyond my years...not only in singing abilities and excellence with instruments, but also in my prayers and songs that come forth. Let Heaven invade me in my sleep, on the way to work, in the kitchen, while the lawn is being mowed....LET THE INVASION BEGIN! Fill my church and this area with intercessors. I declare, "Your house shall be *a house of prayer* for *Your glory* and *Your name's sake.*"

11. Come closer than I've ever thought possible. Let me feel Your touch—Your breath. I want to know You! Wrap Your love around me as a garland around my neck. Let me know how pleased You are with my simple, "Yes, I'm willing to be willing." Do not allow the enemy to stop me or defile me. I say "**No to the forces of evil**; you can't have the singing psalmists, the mighty intercessors, or the worshipping warriors!"

12. Lord, teach me how to offer worship and prayer that is pure and undefiled. Let me *never grow weary* in doing Your will. As a matter of fact, let this be *strength to my body and marrow to my bones*. Help me be an equipper of the saints and a leader of the pack. "You are God and there is none like You." Let me understand this statement and live it out with everything I say, sing, pray, and do. May You receive all the glory, honor, and praise for this in Jesus' name, Amen!

What other prayers or thoughts has this evoked from you to the Lord? Write them here.

_____

_____

_____

_____

_____

_____

Write personal notes, thoughts, and words you are hearing or sensing from the Lord. This may even include Scripture He is showing you.

_____

_____

_____

_____

_____

_____

_____

Prayer Eighteen:
Heavenly Prayers for the Dying, Afflicted, Hurting, and Their Healthcare Workers

1. Father, I pray, "Do not let this one fact escape me: *to You a day is as a thousand years and a thousand years are as a day. You are not slow in keeping Your promises as some understand slowness.* So I declare, "*Your will be done on earth as it is in Heaven.* Let the will of God manifest before my eyes." As this happens, I become more and more thankful that You are *patient, not wanting anyone to perish but all to come to repentance.*

2. I also declare, "*It is the mercy of God that leads to repentance.*" So today I proclaim, "**mercy**" and I also thank You for Your kindness toward me—a sinner and for all sinners. I know *that all have sinned and fallen short of the glory of God.* Daily, I'm led to repent for sins of commission and omission—things I've knowingly done and things that I'm oblivious to doing. Lord, don't let my emotions get the best of me and carry me away to continue in this thing called sin. Don't allow the world to shape me and be swept away to worldly places forsaking the rich heritage I have in You.

3. Today, I'm crying out for my family, my church, this area and this nation. Lord, there are so many hurting people who need Your attention and help—hospitals, medical centers of varying kinds, hospices, nursing homes, and rehabilitation centers all testify to this. As people stream in and out, not understanding that *You sent Your Word to heal and by Your stripes we're healed,* I take this time to call out to You not only for the sick and dying, but for all who take care of Your precious cargo. It can be such a painful and thankless job at times. Other times, the invasion of Your presence is obvious to all and then thanksgiving goes out.

4. Lord, help Your doctors, nurses, and other medical professionals who give of themselves sacrificially to love on Your people. To some it's only a job, but to others, it's the God of the Universe breathing life-giving words and encouragement to each patient. It is also the extension of Your hands reaching through these workers and professionals to people in pain, afflicted by diseases,

cancers, and a myriad of other physical and emotional problems. These are often attributed to spiritual roots that haven't been dealt with and/or the outcome of living in a fallen world. Even so, I declare, "You are in love with these hurting people. You shed Your blood for them on the cross." When You said, *"It is finished,"* You were including these—the hurting, dying, afflicted, and lost. Father, let the health care workers not lose sight of the way You use them for good to help save lives. I emphatically state, "These lives are intended for good to accomplish what is now being done—the saving of many lives."

5. So today, the prayers that I shout from the housetops are for all who are infirmed or involved in their caretaking. Would You send intercessors to stand in the gap to pray prayers that initiate healing? Would You help me lay hands on them and see them recover? Would You allow Heaven to come down and heal these people? Hear my cry for Your people to come forth and see the multitude of needs in this area. Open my eyes, Lord! Let Your people establish prayers for the doctors, nurses, families, and other workers. Send relief.

6. I stand to proclaim that the enemy—sickness, infirmity, pain, and disease—is bound, in the name of Jesus. These things must bow to Your name and the Word of God—*by Your stripes, healing comes.* I appropriate the finished work of the cross to go forth. I take the position of the watchman on the wall, knowing that my position in Christ is that *I'm seated far above all principalities and powers.*

7. I continually give thanks to the King of Kings and Lord of Lords for the magnificence of Your creation. Your mysteries become obvious as they are unlocked to those who study the human body. You give answers to Your workers that are too incredible for words. I thank You for diagnoses that come in the form of heavenly blue-prints, released because of the cries and tears of Your saints. Once again, You are too amazing for words. So, I bow down and worship You even more.

8. My prayer is also for the families who make the daily trek back and forth to hospitals and other places of rehabilitation to help the sick and bless the dying. "God, give strength; send anointing; release encouraging words; allow peace to overwhelm each and every situation. *Allow the peace that passes all understanding* to overwhelm and overtake every person and every situation.

71

Send wisdom, knowledge, heavenly information and revelation to all involved, so that correct and godly decisions come forth. I plead the blood of Jesus in these situations and continue to thank You for Your help." At the same time, I recognize my humanity, along with my frailties. I ask, *"What is it that causes You to be mindful of me?* Who can know Your ways?" I say, "I can!" That brings me full-circle once again to declare, "How awesome You are!" (SELAH)

9. Father, I need the ability to value LIFE—the same value You place on it. Give me heavenly prayers for the dying, afflicted, and hurting—prayers that not only delight Your heart, but bring tangible peace and Your presence to every situation, especially those described as *sickness unto death.* Teach me also how to pray prayers that initiate the ministry You have for every situation. I stand in need of Your help.

10. Help me to know when to call on the elders of the church. You said, *"The prayers of the righteous avail much."* Let my prayers do more than just avail…let them prevail until the greater work—the finished work of the cross—is manifested. Teach the recipients of these prayers how to receive the finished work of the cross! Lord, I don't know how to pray, unless You teach me; they don't know how to receive unless You teach them. What a quandary this is…yet, I trust You.

11. You hold all the answers in Your hand. *Just one touch of Your garment* and I am healed. You did it then; do it now; do it today. Let me operate as an extension of Your hands. Use me in signs, wonders, miracles, faith, and healings. You are the great physician. Let me participate in that facet of <u>who You are,</u> that all may know and give You glory.

12. Father, I've grown weary. Help me in my weariness; I've given up too soon. Give me the ability to <u>keep on keeping on</u>—even when the doctors give no hope. Lord, You know that *without hope, the heart grows sick.* Send me light at the end of the tunnel. Be strong in me and through me. Lord, as I sit and sit, wait and wait, I'm asking You to pour out Your grace so that I can endure this process. **"I am tired; I am weary".** But, *You never grow tired or weary.* <u>Hear my petitions this day; hear my requests.</u> Help me to tap into Your limitless strength. I don't think I will make it, otherwise. When will this end? At the same time, I look for a reprieve; I don't stop fighting. I release peace and Your will…

continuing to fight against death and forbid it to overtake these situations even one day before God's appointed time. I am Your child...hear me today, I pray! Give me grace and relief...Your perfect will be done...not my will but thy will in Jesus' name, Amen!

What other prayers or thoughts has this evoked from you to the Lord? Write them here.

_____

_____

_____

_____

_____

_____

_____

Write personal notes, thoughts, and words you are hearing or sensing from the Lord. This may even include Scripture He is showing you.

_____

_____

_____

_____

_____

_____

_____

Prayer Nineteen:
Caretakers of God's Children—
Including the "Throw Away" Kids

1. "This generation...this present generation...their parents and grandparents...those taking care of Your kids...even the ones in foster care and orphanages!" That's what's on Your heart, Lord! You are so great and greatly to be praised. Your ways and thoughts are so much higher than mine. Everything You establish is for Your good pleasure and the welfare of a nation. You will not let go until You see the work You've begun completed with fruit for all to *taste and see that the Lord is good.* Thanks for not giving up on me, Your child. Thanks for placing me in a family and loving on me through imperfect people with whom I can grow and be established. Lord, I praise You for being a *father to the fatherless and a defender of widows.* You found it good to set Your people in families. You don't want Your people to be alone.

2. The attack on the family is so great. Parents seem to be at wits-end trying just to survive, much less flourish. Lord, do not let parents, grandparents, or foster parents *grow weary in well doing;* but would You remind them to *acknowledge You in all their ways and then You would direct their paths.* You say, *"How good and how pleasant it is for brothers to dwell together in unity."* I'm praying today, "Let it begin in homes...in my home...with me. Then let it spread to all whom I know and to all who come in contact with me. Don't stop until it travels this entire country." I am talking about a nation that has its firm foundation and strong convictions based in the Word of God and established on sound biblical principles.

3. I am crying out for parents and grandparents everywhere. Help women to be in tune with their children. Release mothering skills that help mothers walk in wisdom, undistracted by the tug of the world. Send anointing to aid all who are mothering children—biological mothers, grandmothers, foster and adoptive mothers—so all feel well equipped for the task at hand. Anoint each one with Heavenly information—words of wisdom and knowledge to accomplish what is on the heart of the Father for every child. Place the word of God at the center of their lives;

give each one stamina and determination to go forward with what is right, even though it may be unpopular or not the latest fad.

4. Release parents to much prayer and fasting. Let lasting fruit from this come forth and the difference appear obvious to all. Discharge unity between husbands, wives, moms and dads on how to accomplish this. I release the ability to discipline and raise children in a manner that pleases the King of Kings. Do not allow the enemy to pit one parent against the other. Allow the practical things that every person needs to function in life prevail and be part of the foundational training kids receive at home. **Help all parents, Lord! All need Your help!** Train me, so that in the midst of a busy life I don't forget to teach and establish the things that are most important—the things on Your heart.

5. Grant dads the supernatural courage to be very involved in the lives of their children and to lead with love, not harshness. Allow this love to play out in holiness and righteousness that gains him respect from every family member. Let dads *taste and see that the Lord is good.* From this abundance, let dads impart godly fear that produces righteous fruit that leads to holy deeds that end up in godly lifestyles for the entire family. Top that with the ability to communicate and walk in sacrificial love that is unconditional and forthright—a pleasing aroma to the Lord.

6. Allow dads to walk in a supernatural dimension of fatherhood that demonstrates tangible love to the mother of their kids. Give strong backbones and courageous actions that send the message of unconditional love that translates to children, "Have no fear; *as much as depends upon me, I will live at peace with all;* I will never divorce Mom!" Let this fact be so settled that the "D" word is not a part of their vocabularies. Release respect for dads throughout the entire family and allow moms to model this at all times.

7. Lord, there are people who have grown up on their own... not much input, love, or devotion from parents. Some have experienced abuse of many kinds and most of it is hidden and goes undetected. These children have become, for lack of a better term, the 'throw away' kids. How can anyone exploit, mistreat and ignore these beautiful treasures created in Your image? The hurt and pain from this settles in hearts, making it

difficult for those damaged to give and receive love. It can be next to impossible for them to think of themselves the way You do and understand their heavenly Daddy is crazy about them.

8. So today, I cry out for these 'throw away' kids who are on Your heart. *Though a father and mother forsake their child, You never will.* I trust You to break the cycle and reveal truth. I pray for friends, relatives, teachers, and others to take bold stands that will uncover abuse so that help may be obtained. Now is the time for Heaven to come down and release the *healing balm of Gilead* that will break through to hurting, neglected, and abused people who have been tormented by broken hearts. I *stand in the gap to make up the hedge* and forgive parents who would do such a thing. Then, I cry out as Jesus did on the cross, *"Forgive them; they know not what they do."*

9. Father, how long can this go on? How long can these people survive in this state? I'm crying "Adoption" for those in orphanages and without parents. Mold hearts that will rescue children who need parents. My prayers are for these hurting, lonely people who may not survive unless You intervene. I'm praying that their wounds would be healed and their harsh memories be eradicated by the Father's touch. I'm saying, "Let Your love for people transcend every circumstance and settle on these children, teenagers, young adults, adults, and elderly people. Take away the internal scars they are carrying because of rejection and abuse as children. Mend the hearts of the hurting. Allow the finger of God to touch the deepest, darkest places and let the light of Your presence flood in."

10. I declare, "It is time for the enemy to be defeated and the Most High God to come forth in triumph. Let this success shine forth for all to see. No more defeat." God has set people in a family for a reason and a purpose. Let the reasons and purposes come forth. I decree it is a time of destiny. Let destinies be revealed. Let God's purposes for individual lives come forth. It is for this reason that this prayer is prayed. My goal is to establish on earth the will of Heaven. Use men and women who understand and have Your heart in this matter to take up the mantel of parenting to fulfill this. Help is needed to walk in this sacrificial love. This is where the rubber meets the road in this thing called Christianity.

11. It's for the kid's sake and God's name sake. Release help in a timely manner, that *none would be lost*. Come forth and release the providential grace required in this hour for Your children and their parents. Release godly heritage. Teach parents, grandparents, foster and adoptive parents how to receive and appropriate **all** that Your blood purchased on the cross. HELP! Help is needed, Lord! This is a difficult task. The future of this generation and this godly nation is at stake. I yield to You and thank You for what is transpiring right now as I pray, because my God is alive. You hear and answer the prayers of the saints. Thanks be to God...all glory and honor and praise go out to the King of Kings and the Lord of Lords. For it's in Jesus' name I pray this, Amen and Amen!

What other prayers or thoughts has this evoked from you to the Lord? Write them here.

_____

_____

_____

_____

_____

_____

_____

Write personal notes, thoughts, and words you are hearing or sensing from the Lord. This may even include Scripture He is showing you.

Prayer Twenty:
A Prayer for the Nation

1. *Righteousness exalts a nation, but sin is a disgrace to any people.* "Wake up, people! Wake up and take a righteous stand is my cry. Father, forgive this nation! Does this country really know the consequences of its actions?" So, I admonish all to pray; cry out; seek God to remove the stench that comes from sin. Lord, remove the disgrace that many have brought upon families, churches, this area, and this nation. Annihilate false doctrines and the extinction of divine truth.

2. Who can stand in the midst of a sovereign God and not feel remorse? Where is the godly sorrow that brings repentance? Lord, I release *sorrow that produces* in Your people not only *earnestness, indignation* and *alarm;* but also a *longing,* and a *concern* for the things that grieve You. Grant this to play out in a *readiness to see justice done* in our nation with our politicians—from the lowest level to the highest, including the judicial system and all judges.

3. Let the judges corporately report, "We have done all that we know to do in our own lives in taking a stand against idolatry, injustice, and unrighteousness. We are carrying out the goals of the Constitution in the spirit set forth by our forefathers. Our aspiration is to *prove ourselves innocent* of sin and to carry out God's mandate to the best of our abilities. We have *humbled ourselves, prayed, sought God, and turned from our* wicked ways. We do this so that You, Almighty God, *would hear from Heaven and come and heal our land.*"

4. I declare to the land of this nation, "Be healed, in the name of Jesus. Be what God has intended you to be. Do not back down from being *dedicated to the proposition that not only are all men created equal but are also endowed by their Creator with certain inalienable rights...with life, liberty, and the pursuit of happiness* as core values. This includes the unborn, sick, and elderly. Allow freedom to ring once again so that all may know You are God and there is none like You. I declare freedom in my life, family and church. Let the people of God rise up today and pray the heart of the Father for this nation."

5. *Who can lift up their eyes to* idols and continue the same path when Jehovah God is so in love with me, His creation, and has released blessings in so many ways? Just as *in the days of Noah,* people continue with abandonment and do not seem to take notice of the days, times, or seasons. Let me be retrospective in my observations and not abandon truth. My cry is for people to come forth who will *humble themselves and pray* so that this nation can stand and the kingdom of God advance amidst turmoil, strife, and upheaval. Where are the tears and prayers for You to collect in Your heavenly bowls that many have poured out, not relenting until You are preeminent over every area of my life and this country?

6. I pray, "Release once again the godly heritage that this nation was founded upon. Let that which this country was predestined to be come forth." Let Christians once again vote in godly men and women who are not ashamed of the gospel and allow the Spirit of the living God to bring forth heavenly plans for this nation. I bow to the orchestration of my King!

7. Allow my vote to reflect that my heart is lined up with God. Let me vote in people who will work tirelessly to bring about what is best for this country, not what is best for them personally. Remove the greedy and those who are power-hungry. Bring forth servant leadership <u>of the people, for the people, and by the people</u>. Let hearts that are aligned with this statement, "Ask not what your country can do for you; but what you can do for Your country," be at the forefront of all who run for office—giving freely of their time, money, and life with no expectation of earthly gain.

8. *Can a nation be saved in a day?* I say, "Yes! Let it be so!" I come into agreement with You today and pray for the political structure to align with righteousness and holiness. I cry out that those in office **who will not do the will of God** be removed. Jehovah Jireh, my provider, come forth! Jehovah Shalom, release this country to peace once again…fear must go.

9. I know that the *heart of the king is in the hand of God and that He directs it like a watercourse.* I stand in agreement with You on this and shout, "Direct, direct, direct! Holy orchestration is my cry! Do not allow the rich heritage and providential foundation laid by my forefathers to be uprooted by the wiles of the devil, worked out through evil men and women whose hearts are hardened to the things of God. Lord, if they will not be saved and follow You,

let people come forth who will no longer tolerate this and vote them out of office. Permit their replacements to be hand-picked by Heaven."

10. Do not let the people of God shrink back while the forces of evil rise up to overtake this nation. I stand in the gap and release prayers that will get Your attention. I release the groaning from within that will reverberate in Heaven. This releases prayers without words that releases anointing that breaks the yoke. I stand unafraid and unabashed to state, "This is one nation under God, and I will not tolerate anything less."

11. Therefore, the political structure and politicians must bow to Almighty God. Your arm is not too short. You will <u>not</u> tolerate Your godly foundation and structure to be torn down. God will <u>not</u> bow to man; rather, man will bow to the only one who *is able to save to the uttermost*. Then, I will see the people of God rise up and champion the cause of Christ once again.

12. So, today, in the midst of what appears to be sin and defeat, I shout, "**<u>God is able</u>**! You <u>will</u> do the things You said You will do. You are more than able to raise up Your army in these last days to go forth in victory." (The Bride is listening.) I am putting on my combat boots and standing at attention, ready to do your bidding. I repent for my sins, the sins of this nation and those who in public office have steered the inhabitants the wrong way! Forgive all; come and heal our land once again. I pray this in the name of Jesus Christ my Lord and Savior, Amen!

What other prayers or thoughts has this evoked from you to the Lord? Write them here.

_____

_____

_____

_____

_____

_____

_____

Write personal notes, thoughts, and words you are hearing or sensing from the Lord. This may even include Scripture He is showing you.

_____

_____

_____

_____

_____

_____

_____

Prayer Twenty One:
For the Entertainment Industry and Media

1. Blow the trumpet in Zion. Sound the alarm. Release the angelic host to come and heal...to come to do God's bidding by removing the tares and showing up with God's presence. I declare, "Release, release, release...Let the Heavens be opened with angels ascending and descending today for the glory of God. I release miracles, signs, and wonders to accomplish Your will. Let the people of God arise in faith today to receive all You have for them. I come into agreement with God and declare Your will be done on earth <u>today</u> at _____ (name your church) as it is in Heaven for Your glory, in Jesus' name!"

2. I admonish, "It's <u>not</u> time to stand idly by and allow the devil to beat up on the people of God any longer. It is time to get Your attention and allow Your presence to make the necessary adjustments." I want what's on Your heart to overwhelm and overtake this human flesh that desires to take the path of least resistance. Who can know Your mind and plans? Your friends and the prophets can and do. I position myself prophetically as Your friend, seeing and hearing. All that does not line up with You must step aside. When that happens, heavenly gates open, and the King of Glory comes in.

3. *Who is this King of Glory?* You are the one who is *mighty in battle*. You are the friend to the friendless, a father to those without fathers and a spouse to the unmarried. You are everything to me. You keep me in the palm of Your hands and *under the shadow of Your wings*. You breathe and allow Your breath to cover me. Your joy for all Your kids springs forth when I least expect it. You are holy and wholly to be praised. May You receive all the praise and adoration that is within me, and may I give it freely to You for You alone are worthy!

4. When I look and see *how the wicked have prospered*, my heart sinks. But, then, I *realize the end of the matter* and the end of their story. So, I grieve for them and my tears reach Heaven. You are as much in love with them as You are with me. I hearken to hear Your words. With all that I am, I try to fulfill what pleases You to the best of my ability. I yield myself to Your compassion and Your love. Being full of God, I have You to give away to the

hurting and dying. I see the devastation of the people and cry out, "Help!"

5. At the bottom of this destruction, I take notice that the entertainment industry has penetrated into all areas of life. I cry out for righteousness to have its way once again in the midst of a dark and dying world: *Your will be done; Your kingdom come...* My cry to the Most High is, "Don't allow the imaginations of the dark places of the mind to be the norm for what entertains. Once again, return this nation to virtuous, respectable, and decent living. Allow productions that glorify You, O Lord, and uplift the human soul."

6. I cry out for the people who <u>write</u>, <u>direct</u>, <u>produce</u>, and participate in any way in the things that come from the entertainment business, also including all arts and sporting events. I declare, "Lord, come and have Your way! Come and breathe upon this group. May their gifts and talents be used for *Your* glory and not the enemies'. Come and allow Your presence to overwhelm and save. I release salvation to the entertainment industry."

7. "Don't allow money to be the god that rules here any longer." I know *that the love of money is the root of all evil.* Release that false idolatrous love from this industry. Free the unsaved to receive Christ and escape the miry pit that holds them captive. Let the people of God rise up and cry out for these people who are successful in the world's eyes, but are so empty and are unaware of their emptiness. Fill each to overflowing with Your love. Give anointing that produces books, movies, TV shows, and radio programs that encourage hurting people instead of adding to their disillusionment and misery.

8. Abba Father Daddy, protect the Christians who work in these fields. Guard their hearts and minds. Allow their voices and opinions to be filled with love and compassion. Release righteous words that will penetrate to people at the highest level with authority that can and will make changes for the good. Give Your children wisdom, grace, and peace as they traverse this mine field.

9. Use the saved and unsaved to advance Your Kingdom and uphold Your will. Invade in such a way that Your agenda is advanced without their realization. Stop the forces of evil that have aligned themselves and do the bidding of Satan. Annihilate all the politically correct agendas that nauseate Your heart and are a stench to this land selling the souls of humanity into darkness.

This money-driven way of life, fueled by fear and its forces, must stop. All must bow to the name of Jesus.

10. I say today that all entertainment, arts, and sporting events must bow to the King of Kings and Lord of Lords. None will stop Your Kingdom from advancing and Your second coming. I say the homosexual agenda, the abortion industry, perversion, pornography, child abuse and all addictions must bow to the name that's above ever other name—JESUS! Depicting Christianity in a negative light must cease. All the sleaze that goes against You and Your word must yield. All media of any kind, including the news media, must bow to the name of Jesus.

11. I release people to come alongside the Most High God and produce manuscripts, news shows, books, movies, programs, music videos, magazines, newspapers, internet sites, musical events, shows, and more that will overtake the demonic culture of this nation and release media that will promote and bless this country once again. I say, "Creativity, come forth. Supernatural wisdom and anointing, be released. Writers that have been ordained and destined for the glory of God be established. Godly editors, arise. Actors, cameramen, casting directors, producers, executive producers of all kinds, etc., come to the righteous calling that You have for each. Answer God's call and bidding. Let it begin today!"

12. Rejoice and be glad, for the God of the universe is calling. Step up to the plate and take your rightful place. It is time for all media to once again be released to the light. Darkness must flee. I am praying, seeking, calling out, crying, decreeing, and declaring that *Jesus is Lord* over all media, entertainment, arts, and sports—including Nashville, Hollywood, and Las Vegas. This includes the music industry, books, magazine, newspapers, the Internet, cell phones and radio also.

13. I speak to the airwaves and release the name of *Jesus and the finished work of the cross.* I declare, "Yield to righteousness, leading to holiness. Let today be the day when darkness flees and even the airways display Your glory." Father, I stand in agreement with You and *call things that are not as though they are.* Today is the day *that every knee bows and every tongue confesses* in the entertainment industry that *Jesus is Lord.*" The shift comes and is felt by the world. Thanks be to God and all praise goes to You forever and ever, Amen!

What other prayers or thoughts has this evoked from you to the Lord? Write them here.

_____

_____

_____

_____

_____

_____

_____

Write personal notes, thoughts, and words you are hearing or sensing from the Lord. This may even include Scripture He is showing you.

_____

_____

_____

_____

_____

_____

_____

Prayer Twenty Two:
For Ministers and a Call to the Wall

1. Lord, I know that I know that I know that I know that prayer changes things. So today, I cry out that You would bless and encourage all involved in ministry and especially the five-fold. *Far be it from me that I should sin against You*, Almighty God, *by failing to pray* for those who are helping the people on Your heart. I call out to You today, *lifting holy hands without wrath or doubting,* for the apostles, prophets, evangelists, pastors, teachers, missionaries, and all involved in ministry and their families.

2. Let appreciation be at the forefront of Your people's minds for those that have sold-out their lives to advance the Kingdom of God and see many souls saved. I declare, "Let the praises of God be on my lips for the men and women who have answered You daily to sacrifice their lives to flow in the river of God's calling and anointing. Let many testify that You are awesome and because of You, Your ministers and fellow workers are anointed and blessed."

3. Father, my heart remains heavy as I ponder those who have become discouraged and have laid their calling down for whatever reasons. For some, the attack of the enemy has become too great. For others, the price was higher than anticipated. So today, I release fresh grace over them and call them to pick it back up and begin anew. I release fresh anointing for the situations at hand. I am praying for people to come back to their lives' calling once again. Enter in…the Father is calling.

4. Lord, release the five-fold ministers and their ministry to Your churches. Let joy overflow by having all that is needed in each church to do the *work at hand*. Let this motto ring out, *"I will follow the five-fold as they follow the Lord."* Do not let Your ministers and preachers of the gospel *grow weary in well doing. Let them acknowledge You in all their ways,* so that their paths are directed by You from Heaven.

5. Lord, I have seen the *beauty of Your holiness* and have tasted from the waters of Life. To the extent of my Biblical knowledge, training, and experience, I understand the powers within. Yet, I am well aware of the schemes the enemy has set against

ministers and their families. Father, <u>give</u> courage, <u>build</u> strength, and <u>release</u> the anointing to establish Biblical strongholds for God in the places of their calling and planting. Give abilities beyond their years and grace that extends them into the places You want them to go. Give words that, when spoken, have the power to establish what is on the heart of the Father. Holy Spirit, teach all to be grace-filled and able to freely give 1 Cor. 13 love to all.

6. Many times I have experienced the glory of Your power present in Your ministers. I have also seen You transform their weaknesses into strengths, establishing them as a light in the earth. When others have only seen a shepherd boy, You often see a king—a man after You heart, David, is a good example. It's the same today. The weak and undesirable parts of the body are transformed with just one touch from the Master's hand. Impossible situations... but God...Release over and over again the "<u>but Gods</u>" and the "<u>suddenlies</u>" that all may stand in awe of You, my King!

7. Discharge such godly character and self control that the enemy is unable to touch Your hand-picked five-fold ministers; all accusations against them come to naught. Stop the enemy in his tracks before the assignments are released; send divine, angelic protection to battle and thwart the devil's plans in the heavenly realm.

8. Father, I confess there are weaknesses. Therefore, I take up the mantel to stand in the gap, even when I don't know how to pray, I *allow the Spirit to search my heart and intercede through me with groans that words cannot express.* I allow the Spirit to intercede for ministers in accordance with God's will. I do that today. I'm seeking You on their behalf. I'm releasing heavenly visitations that bring open Heavens to congregations and surrounding areas.

9. Through this declaration, I aim to restore biblical preaching that may not be politically correct but will capture the hearts and minds of Your people, thus, changing nations. I am releasing ministers to walk in fearlessness in the face of adversity. I am anointing voices to be released in the pulpits—voices that will declare throne-room, Biblical truth, even when it appears to be political suicide to do so. I am praying that churches everywhere will be equipped with *all* five of the five-fold ministries and workers will be fully trained to handle all that lies ahead.

10. God, the church must have Your ordained, established government yielded to Your way of doing things. Without it, the advancement of the Kingdom may be paralyzed and unable to go forward in these days and times. This is a critical time in the history of our nation and the world. HELP!

11. I desperately desire for You to release Your glory over all five-fold ministers and the Church. I declare over and over, "*Open up ye gates that the King of Glory may come in.*" You enter through gates that can only be established through much worship and intercession. I'm calling the Church *to the wall* to pray. Forgive Your people for prayerlessness. God, use my prayers and those of the faithful to build the walls that will establish the gates that will usher you through. I stand as one who seeks you on the wall. Enjoin others to this cause, I pray.

12. Jesus, as You sit at the right hand of the Father, could I intercede with You on this topic? Would You give me words to pray this into existence? Would You bring Heaven to earth at just the right time and establish this at _____ (name your church) and all God-ordained churches? I am crying out for You to establish Your heart in Your Church—the body at large. Bring forth the *apostles, prophets, evangelists, pastors, and teachers to equip Your Church to do the work of the ministry* in my day…in my time…for my good…but ultimately for Your glory. Thank You for hearing my cry in Jesus' name, Amen.

What other prayers or thoughts has this evoked from you to the Lord? Write them here.

_____

_____

_____

_____

_____

_____

_____

_____

Write personal notes, thoughts, and words you are hearing or sensing from the Lord. This may even include Scripture He is showing you.

_____

_____

_____

_____

_____

_____

_____

Prayer Twenty Three:
For the Persecuted Church

1. *The Lord is my portion.* There is no other and none like You. The extent of my inheritance lies in this statement. You are my all in all. You are everything to me. *As the deer pants for the water, so my soul pants for You.* As surely as You live, so do I.

2. Every breath I breathe, Lord, is for You alone. I want to be a reflection of Your glory—the essence of who You are to all whom I encounter. **The shout of the King is within me.** All that I need is found securely in You. That fact is overwhelming to me.

3. I drink in Your presence. This pleasure overwhelms me and brings me to tears. Could You, the God of the Universe really be madly in love with me—even more than I am with You...more than I love my own children? How is that possible? I can't comprehend it. Yet, I soak it in, receive it, and dwell on that one thought until I can handle it no more. I am forever ruined.

4. My thoughts and focus are on You and You alone. Who can know You, my King? I can. Thank You for the revelations that You constantly give so that I can personally know You. You take my breath away. As I breathe You in, a satisfaction that reaches to the depths of my being overtakes me. I can barely move; I can barely continue my activity. (SELAH)

5. "Presence of God, power of God, anointing of God...FALL! Presence of God, power of God, anointing of God...FALL! Fill me up to overflowing. Overflow through me to all whom I meet," is my prayer. I pursue only You; then I'm filled as Your presence encapsulates me. Next I'm poured out. (It looks like me, but, all I have to offer of any value is YOU. So I pour out YOU over and over and over again.) The cycle repeats: I'm refilled once again. "Presence of God, power of God, anointing of God...FALL! Presence of God, power of God, anointing of God...FALL!" That brings the shift. I feel it. I sense it. I see it.

6. What is it that You require of me? Is it *to do justice*? Is it *to love mercy*? Is it *to walk humbly with my God*? I say "YES" to all three and make it my life's goal and ambition to please You in all things! There is nowhere to flee from Your presence. You are with me wherever I go. Your grace overwhelms every situation and, with just one glance, overtakes all enemies.

7. Thank You, Lord, for this divine presence. It is available for every situation and every follower of Christ. I pour it out today in prayer for the persecuted church. It is difficult for my mind to comprehend the hatred that the enemy perpetrates on Your people in other nations. I plead for those who have lost family members because they have stood up for their faith. I cry out for those in prison to have the courage to continue on and to **never** reject Jesus. I implore You for those who, in standing up for Christianity, have lost everything and every person who can be named as family. I beg for children who are parent-less because parents have chosen to stand for Jesus and not deny their faith. *Thank You that You are a father to the fatherless, a defender of widows, that You set the lonely in families and lead forth prisoners with singing.*

8. Lord, pour out anointing and grace for the young and old to continue, even as *darkness—yea, deep darkness—covers the earth.* Provide for the persecuted church in every nation in ways that are limitless. Give courage not only to continue standing, but in the midst of persecution to be a witness. Let requests go forward that move the heart of Abba Father Daddy that is seen in tangible ways.

9. May cries reach to Heaven for each persecuted people group and release all to be saved. Make available the words, timing, anointing, and miracles that will change families, towns, cities, and nations. **O God, strength from on High is needed.** Grant eyes to see what the spirit of God is doing and fortitude to do it. Bequeath insight as to how to pray for those who oppress, murder, and persecute. Give Your servants grace to love and to forgive their enemies. I stand in the gap today, forgiving and repenting on their behalf. May the glory of Your presence on Christian faces cause those persecuting to fall to their knees in repentance, come to salvation and be set free from their own chains and bondage...for You died for them, also. Thank You for the sufficiency of Your blood.

10. Father, many suffer in their physical bodies because of the beatings and torture. I plead with you, "Grant grace, not only to endure, but to *rejoice that they participate in the sufferings of Christ, so that they may be overjoyed when Your glory is revealed.* Miraculously take away pain and agony. Send medical help in a timely manner. Provide ministering and healing angels to be released to those who are suffering. Award faith that supersedes all encounters

from the enemy. Furnish plans and strategies that will grow the Church in spite of all that is taking place. Ordain pastors, missionaries, and leaders who will carry out heavenly plans and Biblical mandates that fulfill God-given responsibilities."

11. Father, these are Your children. "Send what is needed for them at the time that it is needed. Give steadfast hearts that continue in the midst of persecution and difficult situations. Hear my cry; hear my plea. Send help, O Lord!" The blood of the saints and of the martyrs calls out to You today. Release the breaker anointing; *open up ye gates and let the King of Glory in.* All of this and more I pray in Jesus' mighty name, Amen!

What other prayers or thoughts has this evoked from you to the Lord? Write them here.

_____

_____

_____

_____

_____

_____

_____

Write personal notes, thoughts, and words you are hearing or sensing from the Lord. This may even include Scripture He is showing you.

_____

_____

_____

_____

_____

_____

_____

Prayer Twenty Four:
Those in Desert Experiences

1. Lord, I'm crying out for those who are in a desert season of their lives. Jesus, as You were led into the desert for forty days, praying and fasting, I understand that You are drawing some into the desert; others have gone there of their own volition. Some have followed the devil—unaware that it was him and the schemes he has planned. So today, I lift them up and cry out that You would be with them during this time and open their eyes to see, know, and experience truth.

2. Father, many are looking for a mountaintop experience with You and instead are feeling alone and shut out as the desert experience has become overwhelming. During this time, be ever so close to Your kids. Allow this desert experience to bring an intimacy that is so close and personal that You manifest how *You stick closer than a brother* at all times.

3. Take everything that began as a negative and *work it together for good.* Lord, release the miraculous power that only comes from an encounter with You. Allow those wandering to accomplish what is on Your heart and to roam no more. For those who are experiencing this due to wrong choices and wrong decisions, forgive them, Allow them to learn quickly from their mistakes and continue on to accomplish the destiny You have for them. For those who have followed Satan into the desert, give time and space for reexamination of their lives, followed quickly by repentance and rededication to follow You.

4. For those whom You have drawn away by the Holy Spirit *to be conformed to the image of Christ*, use this time to have its perfect work accomplished. Permit growth and commitment to the Lord to be at the forefront of all that transpires. Allow anointing and grace to be a garland around their necks, with only the burdens of the Lord placed on their backs. Every other burden must yield to the Lord and be removed at this time.

5. Father, some of Your children suffer from unbiblical compromise and political correctness that come from divided hearts—*tossed to and fro by every wind of doctrine.* **This is not Your plan.** Align each one in Your perfect will and way. Forsake not and allow every wandering to be short—only long enough to accomplish Your will in each life. Help each one relinquish all they are to

You and Your ways during this time. Tolerate nothing to be held back from the love of their Daddy.

6. Lord, help me! Help me differentiate between the desert experience where I am tempted by the enemy and tested *to see if I am in the faith*—and lead me to the top of the mountain by means of going through the valley first. The valley teaches and trains mountaintop survival skills. Without these, my destiny may be delayed. For I know that *without holiness, no one will see God.*

7. It is in the valley times of my life that You train me to be in Your presence. It is during these seasons that the Spirit of God strips away all things that do not *pertain to life and godliness.* It is here that I learn to yield all of myself for total cleansing, so that I can truly *present myself as a living sacrifice.*

8. Once again, I wonder who can really know the mind of Christ. Again, I know the answer is ME! I can, because You reveal Yourself to me over and over again as I travel through the valleys of my life. You reveal the love that can only be experienced and known during these times. How wonderful Your ways are toward me as I travel through the valleys and the deserts in this season.

9. Without these times, could I really understand and experience the mountain top to the fullest extent possible? Could I transcend to the highest of heights? Could the depth of God really be breathed into my innermost being? O God, Your ways are too wonderful for words. I stand in amazement of You again and again. How I love You Lord.

10. Thank You for growing me up in You as I travel through the valleys on my way to the mountaintop experiences my heart longs for. Forgive me for not understanding or appreciating all that You're doing there. Thank You for purifying my heart so that *I can see You.* I do long to partake of the blessings I receive because I know *the pure in heart will see God.* What more can I ask? Once again, as I ponder this, I am at a loss for words. I dwell on it a little longer and thank You over and over for all the work You're doing in me. It's in Jesus' precious name that I pray all of this, Amen.

What other prayers or thoughts has this evoked from you to the Lord? Write them here.

_____

_____

_____

_____

_____

_____

_____

_____

Write personal notes, thoughts, and words you are hearing or sensing from the Lord. This may even include Scripture He is showing you.

_____

_____

_____

_____

_____

_____

_____

Prayer Twenty Five:
Family, Friends, Freedom and Faith

1. Father, when I gaze and meditate upon the Trinity, the thankfulness that is on the tip of my tongue explodes forth from me. I wrestle with finding adequate words for this task before me. What can compare to my God? Nothing! Whose love deeply touches the recesses of my heart in a way that no other can? Only Yours. So today, I adore You with my prayers, asking that You would bring forth from me praise and adoration that is worthy of a King— especially the King of Kings and the Lord of Lords.

2. I hold nothing back and release all that I am to this daunting task. Fill my heart with the attitude of gratitude that would send forth *a sweet fragrance to Your nostrils*. Permit this praise to be my *reasonable service*. Allow every thought and every fiber of my being to resonate with praise to the Father, Son, and Holy Spirit. Let Your *name be lifted high* that all may give You praise, worship, and adoration, allowing You to gain the fame that You alone are worthy to receive.

3. I give you thanks and praise for family, friends, freedom, and faith. Lord, I know that I have a long way to go before I become the person of God You want me to be in my family and as a friend. Holy Spirit, I release You within me to be who You say that I am. *I am more than a conquor in Christ Jesus. I am a priest, prophet, and king. I am fearfully and wonderfully made. I am accepted in the beloved.* Help me to exemplify all of this, especially to my family.

4. You are the lover of my soul. May my family recognize this because of the actions I take daily toward them. Live through me with much patience and grace. Allow this expression to be seen daily. Release the greater understanding of You and Your ways. May this be gained because they see You in me. Give my family and me eyes to see and a heart to realize *the glorious riches of this mystery—You in me...the hope of glory.*

5. I won't be quiet, but continually give You thanks and praise for placing me in the exact right family of Your choosing. I adore You for a wonderful godly family. I trust You to fashion my family into this; therefore, I speak it into existence with this prayer. Even if this has not been the case, I say, "Today is a new day and *nothing is too difficult for my God!"* Even past experiences, bad

memories, and sins of all type must bow to the name of Jesus. *I know that* You are *able to make all grace abound toward me* and give me *sufficiency in all things, resulting in good works.*

6. The friends You've given me are an extension of Your love toward me. I am blessed that You have seen fit to give me just enough—not too many that I would be proud and overwhelmed and not too few that I would be lonely or feel neglected. I appreciate that You are the greatest friend and continue to *stick closer than a brother.* My eyes are upon You as I look at my friends. I regard myself to be fortunate and am very thankful, indeed.

7. Lord, I yield myself to be a *friend to the friendless* as I follow You and act more like You. That's what You would do, so I pattern my life after Your example. Your Word tells me that <u>*wounds from a friend can be trusted.*</u> Since my friends are a gift from You, I believe that misunderstandings and injuries allow the *testing of my faith to produce perseverance.* This *perseverance must finish its work so that I may be mature and complete, not lacking anything.* As I go through life and these wounds bring temporary setbacks, I remember that *weeping is for the night, but joy comes in the morning.*

8. Thank You for all that You allow me to go through. It grows me up *into all things*—in all ways for the glory and praise of Almighty God. My ways are not shielded from You; even in pain and suffering, I will praise You. Thank You for continuing *to work all things together for my good* because *I **do** love You and I **am called** according to Your purposes.*

9. How awesome are Your ways! How incredible are Your thoughts toward me. *I forget not all Your benefits, because I know You forgive all my sin, heal all my diseases, and even redeem my life from the pit. Thank You for crowning me with love and compassion, satisfying my desires with good things and restoring my Youth like the eagles.* I praise You even when I'm oppressed because You are continually *working righteousness and justice* for me.

10. Thank You for providential freedom in this nation. I am free because of the finished work of the cross. Even as our freedoms are disappearing, I know that the blood You shed was not in vain, and the work You've completed inside of me was not futile and cannot be legislated away. *Whom the Son sets free is free indeed.* Thank You for such a great and empirical freedom.

11. Thank You for putting me in a body of believers who aspire to advance the Kingdom of God and allow His perfect work to have His perfect way within them, also. I can't imagine traveling this journey alone, with no help and no commitment from fellow-believers. Even though the Church is not yet perfected, Your Word explains that it is Your exclusive *instrument to speak to powers and principalities.* The Church is still the apple of Your eye and the center of Your attention. *You have made all things beautiful in Your time.* Help me to be a worthy representative and ambassador of peace for You. Allow me to function in a way that continually pleases my heavenly Daddy. Do not allow the enemy to sidetrack me or take me numerous times around the same mountain.

12. I yield myself to You and say that as much as depends on me, I will live at peace with all to the best of my ability. Exonerate me when I get off track and don't exemplify peace to all. Forgive me for not thinking as highly of the Church as You do. Pardon me when I fail to pray and give You thanksgiving for the Church, its people, and especially the leadership. So today, I shout, scream, sing, state, declare, decree, and proclaim thanksgiving to You for my family, friends, freedom, and faith! I especially adore You for the body of Christ—Your Church, Your beloved Bride. I declare for the entire world to hear that You are the head of the Church and are worthy of all praise, honor, adoration, and thanksgiving...in Jesus' name I pray, Amen!

What other prayers or thoughts has this evoked from you to the Lord? Write them here.

_____

_____

_____

_____

_____

_____

_____

Write personal notes, thoughts, and words you are hearing or sensing from the Lord. This may even include Scripture He is showing you.

_____

_____

_____

_____

_____

_____

_____

Prayer Twenty Six:
The Prayer of the Bride to
our Heavenly Groom

1. Let the praises of God resound forth from my mouth that all might hear and know that You are alive and well, living in the hearts of Your people. Your presence is what I long for. Your presence is the desire that wells within me. The thought of You overwhelms me wherever I am and causes me to transcend this world into the next while I'm technically still seated on earth.

2. How is that possible? How does it happen? Only You know. Yet, You are the one who draws me into that place. You are the one who overshadows everything else so that in all things, I choose You! How that delight takes me higher and higher. I yield myself once again. I am a sold-out, love-sick child that must be with my Maker.

3. Who can understand this? Only those who have been drawn into the secret place of Your presence or those who long to go there and be with You can even begin to grasp this. One minute I think I understand; the next I can't even begin to wrap my mind around something too wonderful for words. This is not an illusion of my imagination. So, I wait on You. I revel in this fact. *You are God and there is none like You.* The King of Kings is the lover of my soul.

4. You are the Bridegroom and as a part of Your Church, I am Your Bride. I relish in this fact and try to grasp what that really means. Yet, the words are evasive and I am unable to articulate a feeling, a thought, a sensation, a devotion, or a delight—something so indescribable, yet so real. This mystery eludes me, and yet Your presence is tangible. I can feel it, touch it, smell it, and breathe it. Is this really possible? I say "YES!" The King of the universe draws me away just to be with Him all by myself—no distractions—nothing impeding a holy visitation.

5. This is my cry: "I have to have more of You. I am not satisfied with yesterday's portion. I have to have more for today. Let the newness of each day's dawning bring forth the freshness of Your presence." Even as freshly baked bread comes from the oven and offers the aroma, taste, texture, and delight that is available only

when it first comes from the oven, so I long for the *Bread of Life* to refresh me every day. I long for Your presence to transcend every aspect of my life.

6. Do not let one area go untouched. I yield all to You! Whatever pleases You is what my heart is set on. Whatever is on Your heart is what mine beats for. Overflow me; flood me with the realness of LIFE that comes from a living God. There is so much more. Teach me and train me to tap into the **more**.

7. Allow there to be no regrets when my days come to an end. I choose to know You TODAY so that when I take the step from this world into the next, it is as natural as breathing. When I come face to face with the One whom my heart longs for, there is no holding back—no shyness but only the revelation that I have spent my entire life on that which is truly worth it. I want to know You in the **now**. I want to fellowship with You on an intimate and personal level.

8. That is my prayer and my cry. "I will not hold back; I will only go forward." In the process, I release myself, my family, my church, this area, and this nation to this same knowledge of You. Then, none shall be able to resist the calling and grace of God on their lives. Because of this, *the mountains and hills* will no longer need *to cry out*, for the people of God will take their rightful places and release this marvelous act of worship.

9. Lord, turn my entire life into an act of worshipping You, my King. I cannot do it without Your transforming help. You have all that I need to make it happen. Let my actions be a mirror image of what You are doing and saying in Heaven. Allow me to be a vessel that You flow through to bring this to earth. Give me the tenacity to walk this out with grace from on high.

10. Help holiness and purity pour forth from me like the morning dew covering the earth. Allow nothing You have for me to escape to naught and become a tool used against me by the enemy. Help me not to feign accomplishing Your will in the earth today. It is for this time and purpose that I have been born; I even yield that to You. May the day I was born be sweetness to Heaven's calendar as I participate as part of the Esther generation.

11. Help me accomplish what I was created for. Let nothing escape and dissipate as vapor. Allow all I do to return once again and water the ground of the seeds You've planted through me in the fertile soil of Your presence. I yearn to produce a rich harvest

that the King of Kings and Lord of Lords would take pleasure in. I yield even that to You and Your ways. Let the infinite wisdom of my Lord be a *jewel in my crown that I toss at Your feet* at the right moment. I want to know that I've done what I was created to do, holding nothing back, continually flowing in God's holy stream, gaining momentum in the river of God until Your perfect will is done on earth as it is in Heaven and You receive the glory due Your precious name—Jesus. In Your name I pray, Amen!

What other prayers or thoughts has this evoked from you to the Lord? Write them here.

_____

_____

_____

_____

_____

_____

_____

_____

Write personal notes, thoughts, and words you are hearing or sensing from the Lord. This may even include Scripture He is showing you.

Prayer Twenty Seven:
Releasing the Mind and the Five Senses to Pray, Study, Listen, and Wait

1. Who can know the mind of Christ? These great and factual revelations are available for all to partake. It is for the learned and unlearned, the teacher and the student. God makes it freely available to all who would study, pray, wait, and listen. My prayer today is simply, "Give me a heart to study, to pray, to wait, and to listen. Give me the ability that takes me past the path of least resistance to the place of pressing and self-control."

2. Today, I look to the Holy Spirit, the third person of the Trinity, and cry out for guidance and grace. I have to go beyond scratching the surface. I'm desperate to go to the deeper depths and to the higher heights. My goal is to know the delights of Your heart, my God and King. My choice is to find the threads of revelation and knowledge that are found in diligently searching the Word *to see if these things be so.*

3. My heart is to go past the basics and foundational to the deeper dwellings of water that are pure, clean, and undefiled. I push past and know that I can go there. So, I lay down the things that hinder me…sin which is obvious. But, I also lay down fears and trepidations that keep me closed off from a reality that can only be entered into by faith and giving of myself and time. I yield all of that. I lay it down. I give it up. I press past me to find YOU!

4. I settle on this: there is more, and I want it. I release all of my senses to be anointed by the Holy Spirit. For my eyes, I receive spiritual salve that releases me to the place where Jesus saw what His Father was doing and did it. I release my ears to the cleansing oil that will sustain hearing Your voice and moving on it quickly with whole-hearted obedience.

5. I release even my tongue. Let the *coal from Your altar* have its perfect cleansing work that I may walk in a maturity I've never known, seen, or experienced. Let Your breath blow through me that my nostrils are able to receive supernatural smell that communicates into the natural what You are doing in the heavenly realm. May it go back and forth, back and forth…Your breath breathing through me so that I release heavenly prayers on

earth that capture Your attention because they are sweet smells to Your nostrils.

6. My hands are yielded also. Let the healing glory and heavenly anointing flow through my hands so that the world can truly know that *these signs will accompany those who believe: In Your name I will drive out demons; I will speak in new tongues; I will pick up snakes with my hands; and if I drink deadly poison, it will not hurt me at all; I will place my hands on sick people, and they will get well.*

7. I want more than anything else for You to receive *all the glory and honor and power* that is due Your name. I want **people everywhere** to stand up and take notice of the kingship of the Kings of Kings and Lord of Lords. To realize this even in my own life, I also yield to You my mind. I release it to be in alignment with Your thoughts and ways. I release it to think, dwell, ponder, meditate, wonder, contemplate, and reflect upon You, Your words, and Your ways.

8. I release myself for Your glory and purposes. I get serious about *thinking on whatever is true, whatever is noble, whatever is right, whatever is pure, whatever is lovely, whatever is admirable—if anything is excellent or praiseworthy,* I choose freely now to exercise self-control and force my mind to only contemplate these things. I want to contemplate *whatever I have learned or received or heard from the Lord, or seen in Him*...I decide, with the help of the Holy Spirit to *put it into practice.* Then and only then, *the God of peace will be with me.*

9. Today, I release this prayer into the atmosphere: "I won't back down from intimately knowing all I can know because I have dwelled with the Most High. I am no longer intimidated by the world, the flesh, or the devil. I have and continue to visit places You alone can take me. I have and will recite words that are too wonderful for my mind to think or imagine. These words **will** flow from the throne room and come out of my mouth. I declare that I **will** speak them and have greater understanding because they are spoken. Power **will** precipitate from them and as I participate with You, more and more is given to me."

10. This continues because I choose to give away all You give me to this lost and dying generation—those on Your heart. So, it's at Your bidding that I speak, prophesy, pray, heal, teach, and touch. I don't take it lightly...but I do freely give it. I offer it to all that

You direct me to. I have something to give away because **I've made** studying, praying, listening, and waiting a discipline.

11. This metamorphosis continues on an ongoing basis. This discipline becomes my delight. All day long, I yield myself to become all that You have created me to be. I teach others to do the same. I see the shift taking place. My family, church, area, and nation are changing—one person, one heart at a time. What's more, the Lover of my soul continues to beckon me because He's in love with me and I bring him delight. Wow! The impossible becomes possible. Over and over and over again, I come to Your household to receive what I need for my family, friends, and this nation. Thank You for freely giving to me, in Jesus' name, Amen!

What other prayers or thoughts has this evoked from you to the Lord? Write them here.

_____

_____

_____

_____

_____

_____

_____

_____

Write personal notes, thoughts, and words you are hearing or sensing from the Lord. This may even include Scripture He is showing you.

Prayer Twenty Eight:
Every Day, a Holy Holiday

1. Lord, my delight is in You to do Your bidding and Your will. Allow every day to be a holy holiday in my heart—like Christmas, Thanksgiving, and Easter. May I worship You continually, choosing to adore You with my life. May there be no visible heart change in my passion toward You. I choose to live every day for You, with every breath I breathe and all that I am.

2. May the folly of my ways be forgiven and my heart captured once again by what really matters to You. I shed myself of things that displease You, adorning myself with the essence of all that You are, that this earth might get a whiff of the fragrance of Your presence. There is none besides You. How I long to worship and adore You in the beauty of holiness. May righteousness and justice beautify my every thought and action. May the God of the universe look and know pleasure because Your child has followed You with holy abandonment.

3. Lord, it is You whom I seek and long for. It is You whom I trust with everything. The inward places of my heart that are hidden from all but You choose to adore the risen King, even as I would on Resurrection Sunday. My thoughts are brand new every day, like the dawning of the day or the birth of King Jesus. The brightness of Your presence enhances everything about me and causes others to follow, even as the shepherd and the Magi sought their King.

4. Every moment of every day I choose to walk in Thanksgiving. I do thank and praise You from the inside out with all that I am. I shout it over and over, "I choose You! I choose You! I choose You!" It may sound ridiculous to others. I don't care! I repent for not celebrating You every day in my heart. I repent for not allowing the preeminence of Your kingship to come forth every single day of my life.

5. Yes! I choose to be merry all the time. I choose to rejoice in my Abba, Father, Daddy every moment. I choose to be thankful always! I admit that I haven't done this, and for that I am sorrowful—with a godly sorrow that leads to true repentance.

I have been created in Your image. I choose to be celebratory every day. I will not be distracted by times or a season, as the world declares it.

6. I speak to my heart and tell it to align. At the same time, I choose to live each day celebrating the Lordship of the Godhead like it is at Christmas, Easter, or Thanksgiving. In all things, to the best of my ability, I choose to be grateful. I speak to my soul and command it to line up with Your Word. It will not allow the pantheon of voices to assign its value.

7. It will align itself with the one true God and all Your ways. As revelation comes and truth is disclosed, I will throw off those ideas, opinions, and values that I once felt to be important but do not align with You and Your heart values. I am alive to honor You every day with my life and the way that I live.

8. So I set my face like flint to live in a way that brings respect, glory and honor day in and day out to the King of Kings and Lord of Lords. Your will and life are reflected in all that I do and in every kindness I show. May You shine Your presence through me that the hearts and minds of all that meet me encounter You? The result is lovesick people who are *ruined* forever. You have stolen my heart. It is reserved for no other lover. The deepest recesses are set aside for You. None can pluck You from me.

9. The mystery continues…on and on! What does this look like? What does this sound like? What does this feel like? Since You are new every day, so are the sights, sounds, and feelings that I encounter. My unchanging God changes not—yet You are always showing me a new facet of Your character and presence. How I love to adorn myself with You. I give You all thanks, honor and praise in Jesus' holy and precious name! Amen!

What other prayers or thoughts has this evoked from you to the Lord? Write them here.

_____

_____

_____

_____

_____

_____

_____

Write personal notes, thoughts, and words you are hearing or sensing from the Lord. This may even include Scripture He is showing you.

_____

_____

_____

_____

_____

_____

Prayer Twenty Nine:
Prayer for Israel

1. The dregs of my soul wait for You. I allow the transforming presence of Your ways to overtake and overcome me. I yield even the dark unknown areas to You. I drink in the peace that comes as a result of waiting. Teach me to wait. Allow the strength that comes from this discipline to enhance every area of my life and being.

2. Allow my thoughts to be transformed because I have sought You above all else. The pleasure of this is like a delightful aroma. It rises all about me. It is more powerful than an aphrodisiac or any of the pleasures the world has to offer. Your transforming presence awakens me and allows me to be who You created me to be and not what I try hopelessly to attain.

3. In this yielding I find myself made brand new, changed in so many ways that can only be done by the touch of the Master's hands. It is like the stroke of a brush on the painting of my life— only You can do it. So, I release myself to Your will and Your Kingship. I allow You to establish me fully.

4. Help me to be more yielded and not hold back but to give all that You expect from Your child. Focus me so that I do not get sidetracked or continue around the same mountain over and over, never quite allowing You to be as real in me as You want to be. I declare today that it is time for me to stop playing and engage in the godly pursuit that I was created to enjoy and destined to participate in. I release this continually; it echoes between Heaven and earth. I decree, "Let Your presence, anointing, and glory go forth and do the work that You intend it to do." Hear my hopeful, faith-filled cry today!

5. I choose willingly to forsake the former things in order to take on Your new ways! Lord, establish a nation of people who have the same thoughts, prayers, and actions that align with You and Your word. Begin with me! Help me and all who claim You as their Savior to rightly divide Your Word, so that I know what is on Your heart and mind. Help the Church become exercised to hear Your voice and know the difference between what is real and what is counterfeit.

6. I declare, "Arise godly leaders and don't back down or shrink in the face of adversity or calamity!" I cry out for the appointment of true leaders—apostles, prophets, pastors, teachers, evangelists, and lay men and women—who will speak truth and be men and women of courage with their feet firmly established on Your Word, *instant in season and out,* unyielding in the face of wickedness and Biblical compromise.

7. Give me anointing and grace to stop the cycles of wandering that take me away from Your purposes. I set my face like flint, refusing to travel the same path that produces the same results that leads to hypocrisy and lukewarm living. I cry out also for my family and church. Help none hold onto the old ways. I willingly, to the best of my ability, forsake former things that are no longer Your agenda. At the same time, I refuse to abandon my foundational values which are established to shepherd the new waves of Your anointing and presence.

8. Help me leave behind the sinfulness of selfishness and focus on ushering in Your second coming. Lord, allow this nation to be set apart to You and You alone. Let me not turn my back on the spiritual roots and heritage that were established by my forefathers. Help me not to disown my spiritual legacy and the resultant presence that nations established under You enjoy. Allow leaders to understand this and never depart from Your ways. Forgive me for tolerance that leads to unholy mixture.

9. Forgive me for turning my back on Israel, especially since I know that those who bless Israel will in turn be blessed. Allow this nation to view Israel as You view her. Help me, Lord. It is time that the seriousness of the days in which I live in be considered and examined carefully. Once again, my cry is for **help** in this nation, over this area, in churches, and families. This is a critical time in the history of man. Do not let it be said that I failed to *fast, pray, seek Your face, and turn from my wickedness.*

10. Teach me to love the sinner while forsaking and hating the sin. Allow Your presence to capture hearts and minds; cause the unregenerate and those who are lukewarm to turn to You and repent. Orchestrate this in such a way *that hearts melt like wax* as Your plans and strategies come forth for individuals, families, churches, and nations. Help me to not get caught up in the latest and greatest or most popular Christian wave to distract me from the very heart and will of what You are really saying and doing.

11. Don't allow my so-called *freedoms* to be a stumbling block to those who are hurting and in pain. Lord, help me to forsake my will in the name of love and for the sake of Your Gospel. Help me to differentiate between the two and view everything with the mind of Christ—from Your perspective. Father, forgive me when I've not done this...when the hardness of my heart has separated me from You and Your people.

12. Pursue me, Lord, with a passion that will cause me never to resist You. I need You <u>now</u> more than ever. My heart is pliable. Mold it to Your ways that will impact this dying and lost generation. Even now, I yield to You all that I am or ever will be. Use me to advance Your Kingdom on earth. That is my cry, in Jesus' name, Amen!

What other prayers or thoughts has this evoked from you to the Lord? Write them here.

_____

_____

_____

_____

_____

_____

_____

_____

Write personal notes, thoughts, and words you are hearing or sensing from the Lord. This may even include Scripture He is showing you.

_____

_____

_____

_____

_____

_____

_____

_____

Prayer Thirty:
Perfecting the Saints

1. Lord, let Your light so shine in me and through me that others will see and give glory, honor, and praise to You—*the One who is, who was, who is to come.* There is none like You—none grander or greater than You, my Lord. Let the fragrance of Your presence in me arise. Allow me to drink in the pleasures of my King so that the results may be felt by those with whom I come in contact.

2. I cry out, "Let all the people of God, including me, arise to the newness of this day and participate in the things that are on the Father's heart." I decree, "That which I hear and see will remain in the center of my heart and at the forefront of my mind. Do not allow even a minuscule part to escape from my thoughts, actions, or deeds."

3. Forsaking not the former things You taught me, I step into that which is new—the NOW season in the Spirit. I hearken [listen and pay attention] to realize what is on Your heart and walk in it. Even when the seasons change, I release myself to choose the new ways. I give up that which was comfortable and familiar.

4. Lord, I long for You in this NOW time and season. I long for the freshness of the day. I want to be on the cutting edge of what You're doing. Will You take me to that place? Will You hold my hand and guide me there? I am longing for more of You and reaching upward to receive it.

5. I don't delight that my flesh feels tension in this, wars against me, and sometimes yearns for the *good ole days.* That one fact keeps me on my knees, pressing...pressing...pressing...and evermore repenting. In the midst of this, I have learned to trust You and submit myself to Your good will and pleasure.

6. It is for Your name's sake that I journey *the less traveled road.* It is for the advancement of Your Kingdom that I command myself—body, soul, and spirit—to line up with You and Scripture. My goal is to be so recklessly abandoned that I do not take my eyes from You, *the prize*—not even for a moment.

7. Even if the way seems treacherous and full of danger, I behave like a *good soldier,* obeying my commander-in-chief, Jesus. *I press on* proclaiming truth. You are trustworthy and will *never*

leave me nor forsake me. You will only do those things that are in keeping *with the perfecting of the saints. That good and perfect work You began in me will be completed. Here I am, Lord.* Mold me!"

8. Sometimes my finite mind is overwhelmed by the greatness of an infinite God. As I ponder upon things You've placed in me that are too marvelous for words, I question whether the folly of my prayers will get me in trouble. Lord, I don't want to pray prayers that are *meaningless.* Ecclesiastes states...*everything is meaningless.* I trust You and choose to live my life just the opposite because Your peace surrounds me and You order my footsteps! So I refuse to be swayed and journey onward, covering myself with this declaration, *"Your will be done—not mine."*

9. Lord, give me optimism that I would not grow weary. Sanction my heart to absorb only things that are important to You. I tune my spiritual antenna to pick up Your signals, sound waves, and impulses only. I declare freedom from the trickery of the enemy over me, my family, my church, and this area.

10. Allow me to set my eyes on truth in the midst of 'jibber-jabber' from others and the media that is all around me. Give me the correct focus that absorbs heavenly values and spiritual insights. May I never grow so weary that I give up the fight! Help me be one of many who take a stand and hold on, even when it appears that others are caving in to political correctness and worldliness.

11. May I never give up on the fact that You are a God who loves every person individually and You are able to *work all things together for* my *good* and Your glory. I also choose to remember *that You are interceding for me at the right hand of the Father.* Your prayers assure me that *my faith will not fail.* Thank You for praying prayers before I even know my need. I exclaim to all, "How great is my God!"

12. Lord, let Your people stand and rejoice in You and You alone. As You are an advocate for justice, I surrender to that, also. May Your love spill over to me and through me for the helpless and hurting, that they might obtain justice, also. Allow me to be more pro-life than I've ever been—not just talking the talk; but walking the walk. Permit these prayers to go forth to *stop abortion and release LIFE.*

13. There is no glory inherently in me, but I am a reflection of You— a vessel and a conduit on this earth. Allow Your power to flow

through me mightily. Allow me *to hide Your Word in my heart*; help me *to rightly divide it*. Don't permit my flesh to dictate my future. Assist me in continuing Your path of righteousness and holiness. I hold on to the fact that You are my *all in all*. You alone are the one who is worthy of all preeminence and glory. So, today I dedicate myself to You—with all my actions, thoughts, and deeds. Receive it as a sacrifice that I offer to You, my Lord and King…in Jesus' name, I praise You for all this—a complete work, Amen!

What other prayers or thoughts has this evoked from you to the Lord? Write them here.

_____

_____

_____

_____

_____

_____

Write personal notes, thoughts, and words you are hearing or sensing from the Lord. This may even include Scripture He is showing you.

_____

_____

_____

_____

_____

_____

Shifting the Spiritual Atmosphere

Thirty Prayers ~ Thirty Days ~ Thirty Minutes

Bonus Prayers

Bonus Prayers

Bonus Prayer One:
A Personal Prayer for You (Lauren's Prayer)

The bonus prayers were written for the individual, but may be prayed also by a group. To do this, use the words *us* or *we* in the place of *I* and *me*.

Declare these words out-loud, and see what the Lord will do on your behalf.

1. The Word says that I am fearfully and wonderfully made. Therefore, I declare to the North, South, East, and West: I am Your child <u>and I am</u> fearfully and wonderfully made. I shout it for all to hear. It echoes forth into the atmosphere, and I believe it! Because of this one fact, the enemies of my soul must back off. I say that fear is not my friend; I will not entertain stress and anxiety.

2. As a matter of fact, I choose as a matter of my will to walk out the Scripture that says:

    > *Do not be anxious about anything,*
    > *but in everything, by prayer and petition,*
    > *with thanksgiving, present Your requests to God.*
    > *And the peace of God, which transcends*
    > *all understanding, will guard Your hearts and*
    > *Your minds in Christ Jesus.* (Phil 4:6-7 NIV)

3. As I present my requests to God, I receive His peace. As I receive it, it transcends every circumstance and every situation that comes my way. How can this be? I have, by God's grace, unlocked a spiritual principal, and now I apply it to me. As Your peace transports me to where You are, I walk in a new-found understanding, a new-found freedom. This allows me to guard my heart and mind against the attacks of the enemy.

4. Since I am seated far above all powers and principalities in the heavenly realm, I become invisible to the enemy. He cannot

123

see me, for I am under the wings of the Almighty—so close to You that, if possible, I could hear Your heart beat. Nothing can come between us. This is where I stay wherever I go—at home, school, church, or the mall.

5. Because of this, I have no fear of tomorrow, for tomorrow will take care of itself. I live in Your presence with boldness and grace. I listen and hear my heavenly Daddy whisper words of comfort to me. I align myself with You; there is no place for anxiety, depression, or stress. These three spirits must go in the mighty name of Jesus. I forbid them to manifest or raise their ugly heads any longer.

6. I now walk in the revelation that I bring delight to the King of Kings and Lord of Lords. I see You and You smile as You gaze upon me. I bring joy to the Creator of the Universe.

7. Because You alone are God, I give You praise, for there is none like You, and I'm created in Your image. How incredible is this thought! How awesome are You! How wonderful are Your mysteries and ways! Take me higher, Lord. I choose You above all else, in the mighty name of Jesus, Amen.

(Now, begin to give the Lord praise!)

What other prayers or thoughts has this evoked from you to the Lord? Write them here.

_____

_____

_____

_____

_____

_____

_____

Write personal notes, thoughts, and words you are hearing or sensing from the Lord. This may even include Scripture He is showing you.

_____

_____

_____

_____

_____

_____

_____

Bonus Prayer Two:
Prayer for Protection

1. *Yea though I walk through the valley of the shadow of death, You are with me,* Lord. I will not shrink from the things of God, for Your promises are *yea and amen* over my family and me. Because I abide *in Your shadow and under Your wings,* what can touch me?

2. Though the enemy would try, there is no crack or toe-hold for him to enter, for I am a King's kid, the child of the Most High. *Today I hear Your voice and do not harden my heart as those did at Meribah.* I choose to nestle in the bosom of my Lord and hang onto You as a child upon Daddy's lap.

3. Who is like You? There is none who can compare to You. I squeal in delight as I come closer and closer to You. I do not hold back, and I know You withhold no good thing from me. I rest in Your presence and anointing.

4. Because I'm about the Father's business, I claim Psalm 91 that tells me *Your angels encamp about me.* They minister to me because I am Your servant. You send them to me because I will inherit salvation. I rejoice, for You *command Your angels to guard me in all my ways; they lift me up in their hands, so that I will not even strike my foot against a stone.* I am not naive to the ways of the enemy; therefore I gird myself daily with the armor of God. It protects my coming and going.

5. I release the Word of God over every situation and walk in Your holy ways. My prayers ascend to You as sweet incense; Your presence surrounds me like a sweet perfume. I give You praise and adoration continually, and You inhabit it. What is there to fear? The Word echoes forth that *You have not given me a spirit of fear, but of love, power, and a sound mind.* I walk in that daily, forsaking the former things and allowing You to fight every battle for me and through me.

6. Your cloud of mercy and glory are all around me. You make a plan for me, decree a destiny over me and place me on the path. My footsteps are ordered, because You order them for me. I will not walk in ways that bring displeasure to my King. *I humble myself in Your sight and You lift me up.*

7. I know that in this walk of humility, *You do not resist me, but give me grace.* How awesome this is. I am in Your hands, under

Your wings, and connected in every way possible. The work *You began in me <u>will be completed</u>*. The enemy will not come to confuse, defile, or shorten the walk set before me. *I am blessed going out and blessed coming in.* Your protection is about me wherever I am and wherever I go. You have done it, and that *has me glad*. Let the gladness ring out and the song of the Lord pour forth. Happiness surrounds me *as joy becomes my strength* and fortress. You are glorified in all ways. Thank You, Jesus, for Your mighty hand of protection. In Your name I pray, Amen and Amen!

What other prayers or thoughts has this evoked from you to the Lord? Write them here.

_____

_____

_____

_____

_____

_____

_____

_____

Write personal notes, thoughts, and words you are hearing or sensing from the Lord. This may even include Scripture He is showing you.

_____

_____

_____

_____

_____

_____

_____

Shifting the Spiritual Atmosphere

Thirty Prayers ~ Thirty Days ~ Thirty Minutes

>[==]<

Part II
For Group Prayer

These prayers are designed to be prayed boldly, intensely and <u>out loud</u> in a declarative manner. As you pray, it is recommended that you personalize the prayers. Decree, also, all that the Father places on your heart as these prayers inspire you and precipitate others.

Prayer One:
Releasing Destiny and Favor of God

1. O God, open the flood gates of Heaven over our churches that we might advance in what You have for us during this season.
2. Break off that fear, indecision and unbelief that would stop us from going forward and reaching our destiny.
3. We are people of destiny; so is our church—individual and corporate destinies...destinies within destinies. Let them be released. We bind the enemy from stopping them and release freedom to be what You've called us to be and who You say that we are.
4. We release what You're saying over _____ (name your church)—not what others say! We say, "The church must line up with what God is saying. No more doubt and unbelief... no more shackles and chains...no more financial difficulties, no more lack."
5. We are breaking off lack and releasing Heaven's economy over us. Let the tithe come forth in Jesus' name. Let the offerings come forth in Jesus' name.
6. Wickedness must go. We walk in holiness. We declare, "Holiness today—HOLINESS over our families, churches, and us." Individual and corporate holiness be released. Purity, purity, purity—that's our cry; that's our heart.
7. Let the 'favor of God' (FOG) come forth in all areas of our lives...body, soul and spirit. We refuse to walk in the mundane any longer. We walk in the FOG all the time taking ground from the enemy. *There is a way that seems right unto a man but the way therein is death.* We walk in Your right way—the path You have for us.
8. We throw off plans, agendas, and ideas that are not from You and we choose to align ourselves with You and Your Word. Let us be students of the Word. How we long to walk in truth.
9. We only want to pray what's on Your heart, God. We want to hear what resounds in Heaven. We want heavenly visitations to come forth. We choose to know You intimately...a new level...a new height...a new depth...a new breath. What is it that You require of us? Of _____ (name your church)? Of our families? Of this body? Of this county? Release it, O God!

10. We pray for new waves of Your presence—from Heaven to earth new shock waves that touch us and all that we're about and all that _____ (name your church) is about. We invite You to break out and break into hearts and lives in a new way with a new anointing. We lay down what is in the way and stopping us. We tear down idols.

11. Birth revival through our prayers, supplications, and tears of mourning. "No more delay," is our cry. In Jesus' name we pray this, Amen.

Prayer Two:
The Kingdom of God

1. We're releasing ourselves, families, and _____ (name your church) into Your plan once again—not for the good of ourselves but, more importantly, for the advancement of Your kingdom. *Let Your kingdom come, let Your will be done* through us...so that others may advance and reach their destinies. Help us not take our eyes off the prize—You! We seek You above all else. We're *seeking first the kingdom of God and His righteousness and all these things shall be added unto us.*

2. As the kingdom advances, let many be saved—those whom You have ordained for the glory of God...those whose hearts will be pliable in Your hand...those who will become atmosphere shifters wherever they go...those who have been rejected and hurt by the world and Church but are not rejected by You. Let us, the Church, not reject what You have accepted. Strengthen us for the task at hand. We say, "MORE, LORD, MORE!"

3. Let us walk in the NOW time, the NOW season of our lives without looking back to what might have been. We leave Egypt to enter our promise land of what You have for us during this season. Let zeal and passion for what's on Your heart continue to guide us. We will have no regret for what might have been, living our lives to the fullest today! Make us a people of passion for the things of You! Let _____ (name your church) not waiver in devotion. Let us continue forward in extreme worship and praise that is full of passion for our King.

4. We declare "Let the King of Glory come forth and let Your presence overwhelm and overtake us." We want more of Your presence...more of You, Lord.

5. We release signs, wonders, and miracles declaring You are the God of signs, wonders, and miracles. We decree, "You <u>are</u> God of the healing anointing. Sickness must flee; disease must go; health and healing are flowing at _____ (name your church). Heaven is open; angels ascend and descend for the glory of God." We invite You to "Come, Lord Jesus, come." We choose to make You famous above all else. We lay down our pride, for we know *You resist the proud but give grace to the humble.*

6. Let us take up Your mantel...Your mantel...Your mantel of love. We choose to love with Your love. We choose to love with Your truth. We choose to love with Your compassion. Jesus looked and saw that *they were harassed and scattered.* Let us see what You see and may our hearts be filled with compassion, O Lord. We release our hearts to be compassionate and moved by what moves You. We refuse to walk in counterfeit compassion, which can take a form of ungodly or fake sympathy and even work out in flattery. We shun all counterfeits to walk in godliness toward our brothers and sisters, carrying the burden You have for them. We shake off the lies of the devil and yield our members to holiness and righteousness for the glory of God and His Kingdom! We see the results. Unity is birthed.

7. We do what You say—not what we think. We choose to align our hearts and minds with You and Your Word, not our opinion or the latest fad. Forgive us when we have placed these above your desires, Lord. We repent for sins of omission and commission as we yield our hearts, minds, and lives to You. We turn ourselves over to You—body, soul, and spirit. We choose to worship You in spirit and in truth. Let it begin with us and our families. Let it transfer to the whole church...let _____ (name your church) become a praise in the earth as glory is brought to God and God alone! You are worthy to be praised! We pray all of this in the mighty name of Jesus, Amen and Amen.

Prayer Three:
Normal Christianity:
Walking in the Supernatural

1. Let God's people come forth in these end times to reach the destiny You have for them. Let us go forward with Your anointing to heal the sick, raise the dead, and cleanse those with leprosy. Freely we have received, freely we give. Help us to walk in this with Your grace, character, and anointing.

2. Who can know the mind of God? We say we can because Your spirit dwells richly in us. Because You call us friends, we know the times and seasons we live in. We are instant in season and out with words of prophecy, words of wisdom, and words of knowledge at hand for those in need. We have all nine gifts of the Spirit at our disposal for use when needed. We do not shy away from being used, but go forward because we have exercised them and God can trust us with them. *We do not give up in well-doing but in all our ways, we acknowledge You for You shall direct our paths.* We do these things for Your name's sake...that You might be glorified by our well-spent life. We say and declare, **"You are worth it, Lord!"** How we love You! Help us to love You even more.

3. Jesus, Jesus, Jesus...how we delight in You, our God and King. How our heart beats to be in-sync with Yours. We are searching for ways to please You. Let this be the hour that we look and see, search and find, listen and hear what is pleasing to You above all else. Let us join with people who are so after Your heart that it causes the world to stop and take notice.

4. We say, "In the midst of the battle, we remain true to who we are because You live in us. In the midst of what is taking place all around us we take up our shield and buckler, and our battle cry remains consistent with 'who we are' in You." We don't back down; we advance, defeating the enemies of our soul and those things that would hold back what God is doing in us and in _____ (name your church). We say, "No," we will not back up or give in. We go forward in the will and ways of God. We choose to look with our spiritual eyes, not at what the world says we need to look at or be like. We refuse to be politically

correct at the expense of being Biblically correct. We choose to be a people of the Word rather than those who bow at the altar of worldly opinion.

5. We choose righteousness, even when it is unpopular. We choose the way of love even in the face of adversity and lack. We declare, "You are God! You are more than able to help us even in trying and difficult times." Therefore, we choose to bless and not curse. We choose to believe the best. We speak life with our words, thoughts, and deeds.

6. We believe our prayers go forth and change the landscape of our circumstances, bringing Heaven to earth, allowing this age to intersect with that age. Therefore, we walk in the supernatural, believing that the supernatural is normal Christianity. Everywhere we go and everything we touch is changed because the living God lives in us. We make a majority and are able to change the unchangeable, think the unthinkable, and imagine the unimaginable for Your glory and our good. We now live and think *outside the box.*

7. We crown Jesus king over our lives. You are Lord of Lords and King of Kings. We declare this to the North, South, East, and West. **Who can deny this truth?** *Deep calls unto deep,* declaring "Jesus is Lord." _____ (name your church) corporately speaks the same. We take our stand declaring this day and night, night and day.

8. Sin must flee. Addictions of all sorts must go. We cancel assignments of alcohol, drugs, smoking, overeating, and sexual immorality. Pornography, lust, fornication, and adultery spirits must bow and let God's people go. Since none of us are immune from sin, sickness, diseases or curses, we release these prayers over ourselves, our families, and _____ (name your church).

9. We long to live in holiness, set free from the bondage of sin. We choose to forgive and have our prayers go forth uninhibited. We believe that You have come to set the captive free. *Those whom You set free are free indeed.* We claim this freedom for ourselves and those whom You have called to _____ (name your church). All of this is for the glory of God and in Jesus' name...Amen!

Prayer Four:
One Nation Under God

1. We are a people group whose nation is God. We declare, "One nation under God—from sea to shining sea!" Let freedom ring in _____ (name your country) once again as we fall on our faces and repent for the wickedness that we unwittingly have participated in, including the shed blood of the innocent, and the atrocities against children and women in the name of sexual freedom. Forgive us, Lord, for our silence and lack of action. We stand in the gap and repent for _____ (name your country)—no longer believing the lies the enemy has perpetrated upon us. Help us to turn from our wicked ways. Come and heal our land. That is our cry; that is our plea. Do not turn Your face from us. We are desperate for You to come.

2. We shift our focus from the ways and wiles of the world to You. Give us eyes to see the hurting and lost. Send more laborers for the harvest fields. Use us, Lord. Help us, Lord, get over our fear and go. Let us lead the charge. We have Your heart, Your words and anointing. We are graced with Your presence in season and out to speak what's on Your heart. We refuse to allow fear—fear of man or any other source of fear to grip us or stop us.

3. *You are the potter; we are the clay; mold us and shape* us for the Master's use. With Your strength flowing in us, *we will not grow weary in well-doing, but in all our ways we will acknowledge You and You will direct our paths*, for Your name's sake—not ours. We trust the same for our families and the corporate body at _____ (name your church). We charge ourselves and _____ (name your church) to line up with You that both might worship You with obedience. We choose Your way in all things...all things...all things Lord.

4. We stir up the gifts within us and call them forth. We exercise them and make ourselves available to You. Use us, O Lord. Take us to the next level. We stand ready as good soldiers in Heaven's army awaiting Your orders. Give us ears to hear and a willingness to obey 100 percent of the time.

5. We release _____ (name your church) to be a triple threat in this season. The Church will walk in the triple threat of prayer, prophecy, and praise. It will produce preaching that

changes hearts and minds, while concurrently shifting the atmosphere and aligning the hearers Biblically with You. The result will be that *no good thing will You withhold from Your people*. We acknowledge that God is on the throne and *Your Son is at Your right hand interceding on our behalf.* Therefore, we have everything we need and do not back down from the plans You have for us. The anointing is released over us day by day, hour by hour, and minute by minute. It is fresh oil, fresh wine, and fresh manna for all to *taste and see that the Lord is good.*

6. We proclaim that "God is good. *Our God reigns; every knee shall bow and every tongue confess that Jesus is Lord.*" We declare that to the highly organized powers and principalities that want to rule over our lives, this county, and _____ (name your area); we tell them to depart because *Jesus is Lord* over us and this area. You are the commander of *all that **was** and **is** and **is to come***. We yield to You and You alone. *Let all that has breath, praise the Lord.*

7. Let a holy hush fall on us that even the angels take note of what God is doing at _____ (name your church), in _____ (name Your county), in our families and lives. Let the trumpet sound and the Heavenly proclamation come forth that "**We have been set aside for the glory of God**." Let Your praise ring aloud and many be touched, strengthened, and encouraged by lives that are sold out. Then may all give You glory, for You alone are worthy.

8. We see what our Father is doing and we do it. We hear what Abba—our Daddy—is saying and we say it. We align our hearts and minds with Jesus; Your infallible, undeniable presence fills us. It leads us and guides us in the path we should take.

9. We do not have to wonder what You're up to; we know by the sheer magnitude of Your presence in our lives. We meditate on You and we are changed from the inside out. It is impossible to stay the same; You are directing our every thought and move. We are aware that You are with us, in us, on us, and around us at all times. What can be more excellent than that? How glorious are Your ways! How we live to taste the sweetness of Your presence! How we long for more! We say, "***More Lord... more!***" All of this is in the name of Jesus and for glory, honor, and praise to Abba Father Daddy, Amen.

Prayer Five:
Prayer of Affections for my King

1. Let Your light so emanate in us, through us, and around us that all can see and know there is a God in Heaven who is madly in love with His children. Let us recognize the consuming fire of Your love that surrounds Your people. May we walk in such a presence that people are continuously drawn to us—which ultimately draws them to You. Our goal is YOU and YOU alone. How we long for our hearts to align with You in all areas. How we trust You to finish that which You've begun in us.

2. Let us walk in the salvation that You bought for us on the cross—the finished work...saved, healed, and delivered—100 percent of the time. Change our thinking to align with You and Your Word. May we know Your Word and trust You for the outcome.

3. *You are God and there is none like You.* We declare this for all to hear. We don't back down from our public display of affection toward You, our Bridegroom. We lift holy hands to You. We kneel before You. We dance, sing, and shout in Your presence because we are so in love with You. Our goal is that our affections will be toward You and You alone. We set our faces like flint toward the *soon coming King!* How our hearts palpitate at that thought.

4. So we declare, "*Open up ye gates and let the King of Glory in. Who is this King of Glory? The Lord mighty in battle.* You are our beloved and *You have stolen our hearts.*" You look at us and though *we're dark, You say, "We're lovely."* How that brings delight to our hearts and strength for this day and hour. We don't shrink back because our beloved beckons us to come. We hear You say, "*Come up here. Come up here.*" Our hearts race as we ascend to where You are. We are completely Yours, for You alone are worthy.

5. We say, *"There is none like You."* We crown You King over our lives and hearts. _____ (name your church) delights to do this. The trumpet sounds and we hear You calling us. We tune our hearts into Yours for *Your name's sake* and *the glory of God.* Let the Son be about the Father's business. We will look to see what You are doing and do it.

6. We invite the Holy Spirit to overwhelm us with <u>more</u>. We invite the Holy Spirit to teach us, lead us, and guide us in the way that we should go. Because of this, all we put our hands to prospers. *We cast our bread upon the water and watch it return to us.* The heavenly interest comes forth and we operate in Heaven's economy even in the midst of difficult times.

7. We also walk in health, grace, and freedom from the hands of the enemy. We are instant in season and out to be an extension of Jesus on the earth—*laying hands on the sick and seeing them recover; setting the captives free* with the message and prayer of deliverance; having the prophetic word to bless and encourage as the Lord leads us.

8. Because of this, our Abba Father Daddy receives glory from our lives. We become a walking, talking extension of the Lord's grace in the earth today. Each test we encounter becomes a testimony—each mess in our lives becomes a living message that advances the Kingdom of God. How that brings joy to our hearts because we were created for this—to advance Your kingdom everywhere we go, to everyone we meet, and at all times. We surrender ourselves and _____ (name your church) to accomplish all that is on Your heart! Hear our cry, O Lord. Use us; accomplish Your goals with us at Your side—Your vessel of peace—Your instrument of righteousness, life, and love to a dying world in need of a Savior!

9. We say, "Let that which You created us to be come forth. May the army of God arise in this hour and allow this to be the Church's finest hour." The enemy may try to overtake us and overwhelm us, but we stand firm in who You created us to be. We stay under the shadow of Your wings and in the palm of Your hand. We are protected and blessed everywhere we go because the living God is for us and not against us. You have made us the head and not the tail. We believe You for all good things and receive all good things because our faith is in step with YOU.

10. What can we say? *"Nothing can separate us from the love of God."* We say **"nothing"** because we have chosen to live this life for our King. Therefore, everywhere we go and everything we touch is *blessed. We are blessed coming in and we are blessed going out. The enemy is fleeing seven ways before us.* The things he has stolen from us are being returned to us seven

fold. We are walking in the number of seven—perfection and maturity. For we know that *when we see You we will be like You.* To You be all glory, honor, and praise forever and ever! We pray this for Your glory in the mighty name of Jesus. Amen!

Prayer Six:
Breakthrough

1. Who knows what's on Your heart, O Lord? We declare, "We do, and so does YOUR Church—the Bride who is *making herself ready*." We stand in amazement at You, our Bridegroom and King. We declare, "We choose to make ourselves ready for You." We put on holiness, which takes us into Your chamber. We walk as a people separated unto You, for *You alone are worthy*. There is none like You.

2. The world stands and looks in amazement. When we clothe ourselves with You, we look different, act different, and sound different. The world senses the love of Jesus, yet cannot understand it until they come into right relationship with You. Therefore we proclaim, "Salvation after salvation, new babes come forth. Allow our words to be like *seeds that fall on good soil, producing crops that yield a hundred, sixty or thirty times what is sown*."

3. Make us ready to receive them. You said, *"You lost none who were given to You."* May we have the same record? Show us how to raise Your kids, God. Teach us how to disciple them. For surely the harvest is coming. Prepare us for it NOW! Help us to know how to do what pleases You with every person— each individual treasure that You bring into the Kingdom. Show us how to set them on their road to destiny. Instruct us how to administrate what is on the Father's heart. We trust You for the final outcome that zero fall through the cracks and that our hearts and goals aligns with Your Word *that none would perish but all come to the saving knowledge of Jesus.*

4. Our heart cry is this: *"Jesus, Jesus, Jesus."* We proclaim that name to the North, South, East, and West. We take delight in that name. We stand together with the true Church as one voice to give glory, honor, and praise to Jesus. It is not only us, but our families and our churches. It is for all those who have been ordained for the glory of God. It is those whose names are written in the Lamb's book of Life. We hear You say *"come hither."* So we come. We lean into You. The breath of God touches us and we are changed.

5. How can we stay the same? It is not possible. Because we are changed, it changes our families and churches. The corporate anointing for change brings forth the breaker anointing. God breaks into all our circumstances that we yield to almighty God. Every circumstance bows to the power that is higher than sickness, disease, financial lack, rebellious kids, unloving spouses, marital unfaithfulness, fornication, pornography, drug and alcohol abuse, anger, rage, broken heart, depression, suicide, and poverty of the soul. These assignments of the enemy are cancelled—sent to the pit by the only name that has omnipotent authority to do so—Jesus Christ of Nazareth. We *reckon the old man dead and go forth in newness of life* for His name's sake and the advancement of the Kingdom.

6. We say, *"Thy Kingdom come; Thy will be done."* We decree, "Establish on earth what's in Heaven. Your will; not our will. Your plans over_____ (name your area)…Your voice—Your ways. *Make a way where there seems to be no way."* We take up our sword and shield…putting on the full armor to battle the forces in the Heavenly realm. It is our time to shine. It is also the Church's greatest hour. Let the people of God bow before their King. You reign and rule over all.

7. We don't *grow weary in well doing but in all our ways we acknowledge You* and consequently *our paths are directed.* We understand also that *the heart of the king is in the hand of God.* Therefore we trust Him to direct the king's heart in the path that it should go. Even when it is not the direction we think is correct, we choose to trust You Lord. We choose to bless and not curse. We choose to pray and believe the best.

8. You are the *King of Glory* and we long for Your coming. We long to see You. We long to know You. We long to be like You. Our hearts cry out for more of You and the result is MORE. Our capacity to hold You is expanded. We become less and You take preeminence in our bodies, spirits, and souls. We live for what's on Your heart. We are continually in contact with You. Your presence becomes more and more tangible day by day, minute by minute.

9. Since You have all the answers, we continually seek Your guidance. Things work out because we're working Your plan, not ours. Vain imaginations give way to kingdom realities. Therefore, we thank You for revelation upon revelation. We

see clearly now. The fog is lifting; the veils are being removed; the scales fall away. Once again, we proclaim for all to hear… "How great is our God; You alone are worthy of all our praise and adoration!" Idols become non-existent. You are so huge in our individual lives, our families' lives, and _____ (name your church) life. Everything else pales in light of our God and King! To Him be glory forever more, in the mighty name of Jesus, Amen!

Prayer Seven:
Unity

1. Lord, we take this time to declare that our delight is in You. Take us higher to that place where we can commune more intimately with more passion than we've ever known. Let _____ (name your church), our families, and us be people who are after one thing: YOU and YOU alone. Our goal is that we might know You...that we would sense Your presence all the time...that our thoughts would be on You and that we would be about the Father's business... How we long to be with You.

2. John 17:3 states, *"Now this is eternal life, that they may know you, the only true God, and Jesus Christ, whom you have sent."* We partake of eternity and transcend this world to the supernatural realm now. As we do, allow us to be so heavenly minded that we are continually earthly good. We put into practice all that You have for us. We do not allow the enemy to steal from us any longer. The fruit of our labor comes forth in tangible ways and those around us take notice and give glory to You, our King and Lord.

3. We shout with delight for our heart beats in sync with You. As this transpires, Your delight in us overwhelms every circumstance that comes our way. We become victors, no longer victims. Our way of doing things changes, because we have the blueprint of Heaven for every situation at hand. We begin to walk in the higher ways, since all Your thoughts and ways are higher than ours. We transcend to that indescribable place of going higher and higher with You.

4. The King of Glory receives all praise for the unimaginable takes place and many are changed. All that choose You go from *glory to glory.* _____ (name your church) goes from *glory to glory.* Each family is aligned with the corporate glory that You have released. A new-found unity is there for us to walk in.

5. We declare, *"How good and how pleasant it is for brothers to walk in unity."* We live in a realm of thick anointing flowing down upon us as it flowed down from Mt. Herman to Mt. Zion. We establish a new power grid because we have stepped into

that place where *nothing is impossible*. How can this happen? One word—**unity**. We declare it and release it.

6. We say, *"As much as it depends upon us, we will live in peace with others."* _____ (name your church) lives in peace, and this releases corporate unity. It comes because we have <u>dethroned</u> ourselves and allowed the King of Glory to be <u>enthroned</u> upon our hearts, leading the way because "**unity**" is Your cry—even to the point that Jesus prayed that we would *be one even as the Father and He are one*. We press into it, receive it and our marriages flourish because of it. We declare, "The enemy can no longer assault our marriages or those within our families and churches." Jesus is crowned Lord of all marriages at _____ (name your church).

7. Anger is forbidden to raise its ugly head because that is not who we are. That spirit must flee, in the mighty name of Jesus. We will allow only righteous anger to overtake us. We declare, *"We know what is right to do and do it."* We don't walk in deception, thinking that we're doing what the Bible commands us when we've only read the Word and have not performed the Word. That type of deception must flee. We are *doers of the Word*; therefore our life aligns with Scripture, and *things go well with us*.

8. *We are blessed coming in and blessed going out.* Your shadow, O God, falls upon us and the shadow of death flees from us. Life is released <u>over us</u>, <u>in us</u>, <u>through us</u>, and <u>about us</u>. Your shadow protects us as we lean into Your bosom and find warmth and comfort there. *The shadow of death* has no substance, for it is only a shadow and can hold no reality over Your people. We declare, *"He builds a table for us in the presence of our enemies* and that is where we are seated to feast."

9. Not only are we kept by You, almighty God, and the angelic host, we are protected by the **breath of God**. We hear the wind of Heaven and know which way to turn. We allow Your Spirit to overwhelm us with love. You continually bless us with reassurance and release peace over us, our family, and our church.

10. Therefore we know Your plans. It is for the good of _____ (name your church), our families, and us. *You have plans for us to prosper.* You give us hope in every situation. Even when things go wrong, You are busy working all things together *for our good* because *we trust You and are called according to Your purposes.*

This assurance goes with us wherever we go. We watch as You continually work this out in our lives. Now, disappointment flees, and peace resides in us. Our welfare is on Your heart and mind. We trust You in all things, for *You are great and greatly to be praised! In Jesus' name we pray,* Amen.

Prayer Eight:
Providential Blessing

1. Let Your light so shine before men that all would see You lifted up, praised and adored. We give You adoration for You are due that. The enemy trembles and his minions flee when they see and hear the praises of Your people going forth—the true Church represents You on the earth as Priest, Prophet, and King. *"You alone are worthy to open the scroll,"* echoes for all to hear. We whisper, "There is none like Jesus. There is none who can compare to the Bridegroom."

2. You lavish us with Your love and thwart the attacks of our enemies. Our relationship with our beloved is tangible and personable. It flourishes; along with our families and churches. The declarations of victory come forth, and the *shout of the King* is in us. It cannot be contained or held back. It is like fire within our bones and must be expressed. This creates havoc in the enemy's camp and it cancels the 'no good things' he continually throws our way. How amazing this is! It cannot be seen, only discerned by the spirit.

3. So we cry out, "Sharpen our ability to discern. Give us eyes to see and ears to hear into the supernatural realm. Open our eyes as never before. Let our faith level rise and our thirst for truth overflow the banks of our beings." We believe that in this time and this hour _____ (name your church) and our families are aligning with the Creator of the universe. The domino effect begins…thus aligning the churches in this county and all of _____ (name an area bigger than your immediate area). It goes forth to reach the state and our nation. The riverbanks overflow; Your Word goes out in *power and might*. The gospel is preached; many are saved, healed and delivered. Healthy is our status and that of the people who continually 'walk-out' the confession that *Jesus is Lord* of their lives.

4. Though the enemy assaults us, we are lovers of the Word, being *instant in season and out* to pray at all times what is on the Father's heart. Because of this, our prayers are answered quickly. We walk in the realm that says, *"We've never seen the righteous forsaken nor His seed begging for bread."*

5. We know that we are anointed with the anointing that *breaks the yoke* and fills us at all times with all that God has for us. We have the ability and the capacity to reach up and pull down what the Lord has for us. We have learned to rid ourselves of earthbound prayers—praying God's heart—heavenly prayers. These prayers capture Your attention, releasing the angelic host to perform all that's on our Daddy's heart. Once again, our prayers are releasing blessings that overflow to all who come in contact with us and our church. (SELAH)

6. Without a doubt, we declare, "No contest." You are the one for whom our hearts long; You are the one who leads us in the paths of everlasting life. We say, "It's time for America to once again align with You." This is a country whose founding fathers' hearts were to worship You in all their ways. Even the buildings in Washington, D.C., shout glory to You. They magnify You with words of Scripture and adoration. They announce the providential blessing that flows out from the epicenter of our political structure. Even when sin abounds, Your grace abounds more as generational blessings continue forward and generational curses bow to the name of Jesus.

7. We continue to cry for mercy and holiness so that wickedness would not overtake the national blessings released by our forefathers. In spite of what seems like huge odds, we continue to seek You above all else. Though the tide of popular opinion is against us, we continue to pray, worship, prophesy, and press in. We don't back down or give up. For we know You are the One who holds this country in Your hands. We know that You are more than able to help us in our time of need. We say, "This is the time of need, Father. Show Yourself strong on behalf of _____ (name your nation) once again. Let Your name be glorified from sea to shining sea. *Don't relent until all are fully Yours.*" In Jesus' mighty name we pray, Amen!

Prayer Nine:
Watchman on the Wall

1. Let us rejoice and be glad in our God and King. You reign forever. You are high and lifted up; there is none like You. You are worthy of all honor, praise and adoration. Take our prayers and turn them into sweet-smelling incense to Your nostrils. Let them ascend on high to You, the Lover of our souls. We breathe in, and it is You; Your breath fills us to the fullest of our capacities. That's why we cry out, "Expand our capacity to hold more of You. Let us savor the sweetness of Your breath, and may Your presence so overwhelm us that we bask in the love of Your son-ship." How is that possible? Only You know. Yet, we continue to long to be with You and experience You in this tangible way. Heavenly hosts adore You, and so do we.

2. The ways of the world dim in comparison to You—the joy of our lives. The enemy sees this relationship and backs off. How can the enemy penetrate this love triangle? It is impossible; this love flows from the throne room of God through the finished work of the cross to us and back to its origination in Heaven. This cycle continues on and on. It provides a shield about us, our families, our churches, and all who we encounter. This triangle of love is from everlasting to everlasting.

3. We call out, "Stay near to us; don't allow us to walk a path that takes us away from You. Help us to realize when we're doing this." Our goal is to draw closer and closer. We want our love for You to surround everything that we say and do. Therefore our thoughts are on You. Everything filters through the YOU who indwells us. Our spirit-man rises up and connects with the Holy Spirit. We are led into all truths as the Comforter teaches and guides us.

4. It is our good pleasure to stand in the gap for others...to be God's watchman on the wall...to be a defender of the weak in the courtroom of Heaven and to war against Your enemies. Our delight is to see the captives set free. That is why we stay on the wall with eagle eyes, watching and praying...praying and watching. This will continue until we see You return in glory.

5. How we long to see salvation coming to the masses and the stronghold of the enemy brought to naught. We declare this nation was founded under God and we passionately declare, "Return to those godly roots. Let the church wake up and plead with our Creator to rescue this nation once again. Let the churches open their doors and people rush to the altars, repenting and giving their hearts to Jesus." We release the churches to go to the streets and call the people to come to their Savior. We declare "Now, God; let it be now." We are hungry to see this nation turn back to You. We are thirsty for righteousness to be established once again. We look to You, our Commander and Chief. We follow You and You alone.

6. How we look forward to the day when the Heavens part, the trumpet sounds, and the King of Glory is made manifest for all to see. Until then, we go about the Father's business with strength, power, and might from on high. We don't back off, and we refuse to be offended. We forgive every person who wrongs us or hurts us. We don't pretend that it doesn't hurt; yet, we have made a pronouncement to our beloved bridegroom that You are more important than our hurt, pain, and right to hold a grudge. This allows us freedom to be who God has made us to be. We no longer come into agreement with unforgiveness and drink its poison. We are totally free to walk in the way that holds destiny for our families, churches, and us.

7. Who knows for what we were created except the Creator of the Universe? We will not say to the potter, "W*hy have You created us* like this?" Instead, we will allow You to conform us to Your image and trust You that the work You started in us will be completed. This is also our prayer for our families and churches. Therefore, we are more than assured that when we see You, we will be like You. There is no doubt that this promise is not for us alone, but for our families, churches, and His bride.

8. Joining with others, we go after the corporate anointing and find that yokes are easily broken. We stand in unity, releasing prayer covering and power that will bring the breakthrough. We are no longer standing idly by while the enemy beats up on our families and friends. We walk as *the head and not the tail.* We refuse to be the tail any longer. We were not created to be

the tail. This is not pride, but a reality of who we are in Christ and also that is our inheritance because we belong to You.

9. This reality overshadows every other reality we have ever known or walked in. We are assured from on High that even when the shaking begins, we will be able to withstand it successfully, for we have built *our houses on the rock* and not on sand. Our foundations are based on Scripture and not on some person or personality. We tear down those man-made idols and resist them at every turn. We look to see You and know that the King of Glory is on His way. Just one glance from You will hold us until then. In the mean time, we cry out, *"Open up ye gates and let the King of Glory in!"* This is what we live for; this is the longing of our hearts. Take our prayers, Lord, and allow them to produce those things for which You have created us. We will be about the Father's business and we refuse *to grow weary in well doing* for we continue to learn how to rest in the midst of adversity. Even now Your presence overwhelms us in Jesus' holy and perfect name, Amen!

Prayer Ten:
Islam Must Bow to Jesus

1. Lord, we continue to cry out, "More, O Lord, more." We command the spirit man within to be stirred up and to line up with MORE. Our spirit connecting with Your spirit is what we're longing for. Otherwise, dead works that cause us to step out of Heaven's realm come forth and we operate in the flesh. We crucify our flesh, because we want to be with You...in Your presence.

2. Holy Spirit take us to that place where the longing of our hearts intersects with Heaven and Your will is released over us. Corporately, _____ (name your church) walks in this heavenly intersection and brings the will of God to earth. The unction is for the corporate church and us, also. This produces overflow that floods this community as we help take it for Jesus.

3. We are forsaking the old ways—the way we've always done things. We position ourselves for all that You have for us. We long for just one glimpse of You...to feel Your presence. We're like *the deer that pants for water* in a dry and thirsty land, longing to touch You. We go into that secret place where sin and lust can't exist, and there You are *in all Your goodness and majesty.* We long to see You with our eyes and experience You in this life—in the land of the living.

4. Declarations come forth from our lips that say, "**Now** is the time for You to be made famous throughout the entire earth. **Now** let the people groups all over the world hunger and thirst for You to show Yourself strong on their behalf...for Your name is to be glorified forever." We shout, sing, declare, and boast in You and You alone. When we do that, everything pales in light of the majesty of Your omniscient, omnipotent, omnipresent ways. The world bows before their King and shouts, *"Hosanna! Hosanna! Hosanna!"*

5. We say Islam must bow to the name of Jesus. We choose to love the Islamic people, as God does, for "God so loved the world", but we refuse to prostitute ourselves with the spirits behind Islam. We choose not to come into alignment with its violence and abuse. Filled with righteous anger, we shout,

" _____ (name your nation) will not be one nation under Allah. The spirits behind this Islamic march on _____ (name your nation) must flee, in the name of Jesus. We forbid these spirits to plant themselves on our soil and in the hearts of our men, women, and children." We decree, "Let the praying church arise and overwhelm this power of darkness."

6. We stand and boldly declare "NO" to the Imams and clerics of Islam who have declared a holy jihad on all unbelievers or infidels. We bind up the murder and violence that go along with this belief system. We break off the lie of the devil that this assures the Muslims a place in Heaven. We join ranks with Christians everywhere who are taking a stand against this deception, praying that their eyes would be open and that *many would come to the saving knowledge of Christ.*

7. We are determined to vote out politicians who stand on the side of political correctness and tolerance at the expense of truth, justice, and righteousness. We agree with scripture that says, *"Righteousness exalts a nation, but sin is a disgrace to any people."* Our prayers go forth to stop sin in its tracks and will not allow this disgrace to be upon us any longer. We magnify the righteousness of Christ and come into agreement with all that His shed blood accomplished for humans everywhere.

8. We are Christians who will not be easily persuaded, deceived, or lulled to sleep. The sleeping giant of the church awakens from its slumber and cries out, "**No more!**" We, along with our fellow-believers, draw a line in the sand and say, "It stops here—no further. You cannot have this nation! You won't infect our families or friends with Your rhetoric *of peace when there is no peace."* We stand in the gap to repent for this nation—from the highest level of government to the lowest—for entertaining ungodliness in any form. We will not turn a blind-eye to the news media with their outright lies and deception. We trust the One who is faithful to stop it in its tracks. We release the angelic host to fight this battle alongside us. *Our God reigns* will be the outcome of all this. To You be all glory, honor, and praise forever and ever! It's in Jesus' name that we release this, Amen.

Prayer Eleven:
Breaking Curses, Releasing Blessing

1. Let hearts, minds, and spirits in the people of this nation align for God's glory and good pleasure. We **now** come into agreement with the reason for our existence...to bring glory to our King...to know You, love You, and serve You forever. *Every knee will bow; every tongue will confess that Jesus is Lord.* Our confession of faith makes darkness flee—light drives it away. All will know Your ways are majestic, O Lord. How awesome are Your thoughts toward us. How incredible that One such as You would even notice us!

2. *Your mercy endures forever.* Divine mercy is bestowed on believers and unbelievers alike, *for You show no favoritism.* (*You rain on the just and the unjust.*) We walk in this great mystery, and our hearts beckon us to partake. Yet, if we're not careful, this could be missed—looking for love in all the wrong places. The enemy of our soul and the one who comes to steal our destiny makes sure of this. He blinds us and slimes us with unexpected situations. Yet the One we were created for continues to bid us *come up higher.* Come up here.

3. The Word tells us (Isa 30:21), *"Whether you turn to the right or to the left, your ears will hear a voice behind you, saying, 'This is the way; walk in it.'"* So we listen and step out to do what You are telling us. Our spirit soars as it comes into agreement with this. There is no other way to go but up...higher and higher... fuller and fuller...richer and richer in the knowledge and ways of God. We experience daily that which we had only read about or heard that others had walked in. Visions, trances, dreams, and prophesies—all of the supernatural—become our way of life. Walking on earth with our antennas in Heaven becomes the norm.

4. We declare, *"We know what is right to do and do it."* Yet, we also know in the last days *wrong will be called right* and *right will be called wrong.* We shout to the North, South, East, and West, **"What is wrong with right?"** The corporate Church takes its stand and does not bow to iniquity and perversity. We set our hearts to hate evil with a perfect hatred and trust God to turn

this nation back to righteousness. Our trust is in You, our King, knowing that *You are more than able.*

5. We speak to mountains of poverty, spiritual lack, selfishness, unbelief, immorality, addiction, and pride. We command them to be cast into the sea. Our mustard seeds of faith are more than sufficient to accomplish this. We agree *as in touching* and see You, our Lord and Savior, set us free from any crises at hand.

6. Those who are *weak become strong,* walking in *the power of Your might*—not the arm of flesh. This breaks off curses that come from trusting in the arm of the flesh. We have a new-found freedom that superimposes upon us things that *eye has not seen, nor ear heard, neither have entered into the heart of man what God has prepared for us that love You.* How awesome is this! (SELAH)

7. We say we will not *let our hearts be troubled; neither will we let them be afraid. We have chosen to put our trust in You* and You are unable to disappoint us. For we know *You reign* in all circumstances—past, present, and future. As we *plead the blood* that Jesus shed for us and walk in the finished work of the cross, we see and experience that *no weapon formed against us has legal right to prosper.* We have pulled the rug out from the enemy and stripped him of all legal access to our lives.

8. Because of this, we now see that the *words of our mouth and the meditations of our heart are pleasing to* God; what else can they be? We stand in the gap canceling every hex, vex, incantation, evil surmising, witchcraft prayer, and word curse ever spoken about our churches, families, or us. We annihilate them in the name of Jesus and say, "They are null and void as if never spoken."

9. We meditate on Scripture and trust You to *watch over Your Word to perform what is on Your heart concerning us.* Therefore we walk in generational blessing and prosperity of the body, soul, and spirit. Everything we touch is blessed; everywhere we walk is ground taken for the Kingdom. Our belief system, based on the Word of God—the Holy Inspired Scriptures, is now our reality forever and ever in Jesus' holy name, Amen and Amen!

Prayer Twelve:
That We Might Know You

1. Hearken! Alas! You draw near to Your children. Your right hand of blessing reaches forth and so does Your left hand of judgment...Blessings overtake those who do Your will and accomplish Your bidding. The left hand is there for those who refuse this. Yet the cry of our hearts continues to be "mercy, mercy, mercy"! What else are we to say except "mercy"? For *Your mercy is new every morning* and it endures forever. Generational blessings go forth for a thousand generations to those who obey You and uphold Your commands.

2. The light of Your love shines forth into the darkness, and it flees. The generations advance in blessing because of the overwhelming love of Your virtue that adorns them. We take refuge in You. Our delight to do Your will remains our highest priority. The *Lamb of God who takes away our sin* releases all that we need for every situation. We sit with You and find the greatest contentment of our hearts. All longings, desires, and wants are fulfilled in You. (SELAH)

3. We don't let mere facts get in the way of truth and reality. As we enter into that higher reality, we ignore facts on our quest for truth. Your ways are true. Your thoughts remain at the front of all we do and say. This stuns us and we awaken to the change that brings delight to Your heart. We adorn ourselves with the pleasures that come from holy and righteous living. We proudly wear You like a mantel for all to see.

4. Because we are still *in the world, but not of the world,* as we are interacting with those around us, the result is they receive a touch from You just by being near us. (We can barely grasp this mystery.) How great are Your ways! We can only imagine things so wonderful; yet, our hearts yearn for this like a nursing baby longs for its mother's milk.

5. That we might know You! That is the cry of our hearts, O Heavenly Daddy! That we might know You and walk in Your ways...that Your presence fills us and overwhelms us. We sit beside You and ponder, "Is it possible to be with You in Your presence and not be changed? NO! Is it possible to enter into that unknown realm and remain the same? NO!" This thought

157

overtakes us and possibilities become reality. Even our DNA changes for good.

6. Our plea is simple: "Continue to reveal Yourself to us. Bring forth the revelations of Your heart. Release it for this dying generation that has departed from Your ways and refuses to consider Your thoughts." Oh, Lord, how can one so awesome and majestic be ignored? Since this possibility advances toward reality, we pray, "Never Lord, never."

7. How do we communicate You to unbelievers, atheists, agnostics, and pagans? Give us words that penetrate to the heart so that none can resist You. Let our connection with You be so strong, yet so sweet, that Your words are always on the tip of our tongues ready to be spoken—like *apples of gold in settings of silver.* Our thoughts replaced by Yours—Heavenly thoughts that transcend this world to produce words that yield kingdom decisions on behalf of the unsaved.

8. Our loud cry penetrates the atmosphere, "Stir things up. Turn this world upside down for Jesus. Tear down the kingdom of darkness. Reveal the Bride of Christ. Advance the Kingdom of God! <u>Charge</u>!" Don't stop until *Your Kingdom comes; Your will is done on earth as it is in Heaven.*

9. Break up the fallow ground of the hearts of Your people. Cause them to be pliable before You. Take us at our word and release the secret weapons of our warfare—love that produces forgiveness and brings repentance. We commit to stand in the gap and make up the hedge for hundreds, thousands, tens of thousands and more. We know that *one can put a thousand to flight and two—ten thousand.* How is this possible? Yet, we believe for it. Once again we yield to the upside down Kingdom that holds life everlasting for all and remains a mystery. Let God be praised forever, in Jesus' name, Amen!

Prayer Thirteen:
Awaken Church!

1. How can we reach the heights of Heaven where You rule and reign? How do we get to where You are? Take us there. That is our heart's cry. We look to see You; we seek to find You; we reserve this time just for You. No other focus, no other interruption—just You and us. Let that heavenly presence melt over us. We soak and bask in You and You alone. We don't give up, for we know that when *we seek You, we will find You.* We hear, *"Be still and know that I Am God."*

2. So in the quiet, our hearts wait and rejoice in the pleasure of You—our King. The delight that we draw is strength to our being and life-giving breath. Without it we would suffocate. As we lay in Your arms, soaking up the love of our Bridegroom, we hear the beat of Your heart for Your people around the world.

3. It brings us back to reality as we sense Your sadness and love for the lost, hurt, dying, and oppressed. This strengthens us for the battle at hand. The intensity of the moment explodes with purpose. For this we were born…to enter into the fight for all that really matters—the Kingdom of God, eternity, bringing Heaven to earth, and aligning ourselves, families, churches, this area, and this nation with Your purpose and plan.

4. So again, we cry out, "Awaken, church, awaken!" to the God of the universe…to Your purposes and plans. How much time must pass before our eyes are focused on what God focuses on?" Now is the time Lord; allow us to see You in Your glory. Let us go about the business of seeing many saved and made disciples of the Most High God.

5. Help us see the church emerge once again with Holy Spirit convictions, not swayed *by every wind of doctrine, but able to rightly divide the word of God.* Then and only then will the world arise and take notice. They will exclaim, **"Surely God is in this place."** An explosion from on high will target and regenerate hearts and minds, advancing the kingdom of God one person, one soul at a time. How our hearts long for this.

6. If You would tarry too long, all would seem lost. But we know You are God and You hold time in Your hands. We praise You that things happen in Your time, in Your way, and *for Your good*

pleasure. Every trial and tribulation bows to You, our King. Without a doubt, all things bow to You—even the systems of the world.

7. Every political official and judge, from the highest to the lowest, is responsible and answers to You. Babylon, the great harlot; the world's financial institutions must bow to Jesus. Thank You for holding it all in Your hands. Many are counting the cost of what their lives have amounted to, as some have *built their house on sand* instead of the rock. They now realize that the result has been that *all is vanity.*

8. We cry for "accountability and blessings. Stinginess, selfishness, pride, self-importance, envy, self-reliance and jealousy must go." In its place we declare, "godliness, freedom, holiness, generosity, humility, hard-work, perseverance, and fortitude." The church arises to take back what is rightfully hers. In the midst of suffering and lack, it is her finest hour.

9. The people of God arise and receive *the mammon from the wicked that has been stored up for the righteous.* You, the King of the Ages, prove Yourself faithful once again as we call upon You in our times of need and desperation. You hear and answer. This echoes throughout the whole earth as people are drawn to You. The Word tells us that *when You are lifted up* (in good or bad times), *You draw all men unto Yourself. That sounds like change to us—real, anointed, and unadulterated change that takes place in the heart and connects with the mind; bringing forth body, mind, and spirit that align with the King of Glory.* Release this plus more O Lord, in Jesus' mighty name we pray, Amen!

Prayer Fourteen:
Strengthening Marriage to
Break-Free from Divorce

1. It is never too late to release the greatness of God over the situations at hand. Lord, You *never tire or sleep*. Because of Your omnipotent nature, we trust You with all things. Nothing is too difficult for You—absolutely nothing. That's why strangers adore You. We wrap ourselves around You and choose not to let go. We know the ride ahead is more marvelous because we're intentional in the things we do—choosing to place You in the center of everything. Your ways overwhelm us and become a fragrance that beckons us to You. We are not silenced by the nay-sayers, because You have our rapt attention.

2. We take a stand, praying fervently, "Forgive America for its lax stance on pornography, the sexual slave trade, and abortion." Just because we haven't seen it taking place doesn't mean You don't. Just because we don't feel the pain first-hand doesn't mean You don't. "Break our hearts with what breaks Yours, Lord. Remove the walls, the scales, and the hard crust from our hearts that blocks us from this."

3. Lord, *against You and You alone have we sinned*. Constantly we observe sin that plays out in lack of love and commitment to the marriage covenant. This causes divorce rates to soar and children to suffer without both of their parents in the home. The hurt and pain is then put on display for the world to see as case after case goes before a judge and the judicial system intervenes with orders that may or may not release God's will for each family. This tragedy must be abated!

4. Stop it in its track and turn the hearts of Your people back to their spouses. We release devotion over marriages—our marriages (or future marriages). Give us a heart that has passion for the one with whom we made (or will make) a covenant. Let us not lose sight of Your plan for our lives and how it interconnects with our spouses (or future spouses). We bless our spouses (or future spouses) with every good thing. We declare, "Faithfulness, love, and the ability to go the extra mile." We make a demand on the anointing for all marriages. "Release more grace," we pray. We

remain unsatisfied until You invade Your presence into every aspect of our lives, marriages, and families. We declare victory over the enemy, commanding him to **"back off"**. We release angels to minister in the areas where we fall short. "Help us, Lord!" That is our cry.

5. Lord, Your Word tells us that You *hate divorce*; we understand why. Your children are overwrought with suffering resulting from the anger, rage, hurt, rejection, and pain of this stench. What does this broken covenant teach the children? What message are they receiving? How does this play out in their lives? Could it be that this results in addictions, mental and physical illness of all kinds, rebellion, depression, and sexual immorality? Where are the stalwarts that will cry out for these hurting, broken people? Who will even notice?

6. Our cry today is "Help! O Lord; forgive this nation and its people for willing and unrighteous participation in divorce. *Make a way where there seems to be no way*; break off this generational curse. Rise up and defend the defenseless; rise up and empower those who are downtrodden under this adversity and travesty. Provide judges that will make righteous decrees in the face of this. Empower them with grace from on high to go against the tide of popular opinion so that Your people can remain afloat and their children can persevere when all is against them and their lives are crashing in. Help in this dark hour, Lord; our cry is for help!"

7. Lord, we pray for those who have innocently participated in divorce—not knowing any better...or prior to their salvation. Lord, remove the scars, guilt, and shame that so many continue to carry as the enemy reminds them of their past. Help them receive the love and mercy that God freely gives them as children of the Most High. We release the fragrant incense from the throne that reminds us *there is no condemnation in Christ Jesus.*

8. Forgive this nation for allowing drug addiction, alcohol abuse and addictions of all sorts to become rampant and the grief that accompanies this—especially since it often begins at a very young age. What is this teaching children and this generation? It tears apart families bringing guilt, shame and destruction. It even robs kids of their youth and continues to steal from them in middle age only to bring horrific and untimely death. If death

does not come prematurely, the suffering continues like clockwork into old age, leaving people ravished in every area of their lives—without health, the love of family members or friends, and penniless. This is the work of the one who has come *to rob, kill, and destroy.* Use these words to halt this, we pray!

9. Television shows and movies depict this with frivolity and light-heartedness—trivializing its sinfulness and its outcome. Teenagers become hardened to this and believe it to be normal. Forgive! Lord! This is **NOT** who You created us to be! That cry swells from the depth of Your being to us…the intercessor within screams for "justice and relief. Where are the people of God with righteous indignation?" Bring us back to the basics.

10. Therefore, our cry is for help and intervention. The orphaned generation that falls prey to this is pitied, but left to find their way all alone; few bother to care, most pretend not to notice. Yet, we know that You love them and feel their hurt and pain, even though they may no longer be a functioning part of society and so conveniently take their places in the ranks of one more victim of Satan and his demons. Lord, teach us to pray for this hurting group of people. Show us how to love them not only with our prayers, but also with our actions…in Jesus' consuming and compassionate name, Amen.

Prayer Fifteen:
Prodigals, Burnt Stones, the Forgotten, and the Hidden

NOTE: The term **burnt stones** mentioned in the first paragraph below was coined by someone in a prayer meeting I attended. It speaks of people who have been hurt or burned by the Church. It can also refer to wounded warriors—those with battle scars received in the spiritual line of fire.

1. Lord, we're praying for people who have lost their way— prodigals, burnt stones, the forgotten, and the hidden. We sense their pain and look to see who will cry out for them. Who will call their name before the throne of grace? In this place of desperation, who will stand in the gap between the porch and the altar shedding tears for them? Here we are, Lord; use us. Allow our prayers to echo in the heavenly chamber and court room.

2. We say, "It is time for them to grab hold of their destinies, for the enemy to stop harassing them, and for their spirit-man within to rise up." Hold on for the ride; the King of Glory comes to the rescue. Don't relent until the hidden and hurting ones are again fully Yours, Lord. Take away that which hinders. Open eyes to the higher reality—Your will and Your ways.

3. We see the dungeons in which circumstances and bad decisions have placed people. We understand the pit that's been dug. "Is it possible to escape?" is their cry. You hold the answer; You hold the key. If this is not the situation, show what is taking place. If You are holding them captive for Your greater purposes, make it evident to each. So today, we set aside this time and allow the key of prayer to echo forth that You would have mercy, cancel the assignments of the evil one, and send the angelic host to defend the hurting, hopeless ones.

4. His forces seem to be laxly arrayed, for there has been little warfare on their behalf. Seemingly with ease, he has held the captives in captivity, lulling many to sleep; most have lost desire to fight any longer. So, we call out, "Awaken! Align once again with the Kingdom of God. Allow God's army angels to come and rescue. Do not align any longer with luke-warmness

and life patterns that hold many in status quo." Today we declare, "Break-through and break-out."

5. Release the Esther, Joseph, and Joshua generation to receive divine revelation to their calling. Help us understand our anointing *for such a time as this*. We set aside time to release prayers that echo throughout Your throne room that You would have mercy and send Heaven's angels to minister to the prodigals and hidden ones. Bring divine revelation. Cancel assignments the evil one has lobbied against this entire group of Your hurting children. Release this Papa Daddy/Abba Father, we pray.

6. *God, You are not a man that You should lie.* You have come to set the captives free. So, we release a prayer of breakthrough that allows break-out of Your prodigals and burnt stones. Remove their hurt, O Lord; remove their pain. Let the injustices be accounted for and the court room of Heaven convened for the taking back of what the enemy has stolen. Today is the day of receiving seven times what has been taken. We say, "Let it be today...for their good and Your glory." We fight in the heavenly realms, tearing down strongholds, appropriating what and who they are in Christ...no longer held captive by the enemy. We understand that You not only promise, but You also deliver!

7. We hear the cries of the hurting, "But God, we've done all we know to do. What else are we to do? *If You but say the word, Your servant would be healed.* We can only do what we know to do. Teach us O Lord; help us. We're desperate. **Do You hear us**? **Where is the answer**? We have set our faces as flint. *Though You slay us, yet will we serve You. We will not grow weary in well-doing. We're choosing to acknowledge You in all our ways.* Please hear our cries. *Direct our path* and it shall be directed. We give You permission. Do whatever it takes that we might hear You. Our only desire is to obey You. How we long for You; how we thirst for You in this dry land. When will this end?"

8. Lord, teach us how to minister to these, the hurting. Send more to minister. More ministers are needed. Turn all that love You into walking, talking ministers of the gospel of Jesus Christ. Show us how to walk in the fullness of the cross, giving away the total package—saved, healed, and delivered. Give us the

right words to say—words that will reach into the depth of their beings to release Your kindness and love for them.

9. We choose Your ways in this land that reeks desolation for many. In the midst of this, we continue to believe that *we are more than conquerors in You and Your grace is sufficient for us. Nothing can separate us from You...not death nor life...not angls nor powers or principalities...not things in the present nor things to come...* not even divorce, addictions, hurt or pain. Thank You for Your great abounding love that won't allow us to be separated from You. What does that look like? What does it sound like? What does it feel like? We yield ourselves to You and say, "Let it come forth, guiding our lives at all times so that our paths continue to be straight—*walking the narrow path...running the race* You have *set before us.* All that we are or ever hope to be, we yield to You. We are Your vessels, O Lord. We are Yours...We are Yours...We are Yours...We beseech You, O Lord, in Jesus' name, Amen.

Prayer Sixteen:
A Prayer of Worship, Adoration, and Obedience

1. "Awake! Awake! O sleeper...for the time has come and now is for true worshippers to worship God in *spirit and in truth.*" It is time for You to receive the worship and adoration we long to give You and that You deserve. You call out to the worshippers, "Come." Do we hear You calling? Do our hearts alight with Your presence when You call to us? Yes, it does, for we long to love on You.

2. Help us Lord! We don't know how to do this. Teach us; show us; equip us so that the longing within can be satisfied. We are a vehicle and a conduit of worship. We release this for us, our families, our churches, this county, state, and nation. Teach us how to love on You through worship. Begin with us. We release ourselves today. Grow us up in true worship, Lord. Because of Your *great mercy; we freely choose to offer our bodies as a living sacrifice—our spiritual act of worship to You—our reasonable service. We're choosing to be transformed by the renewing of our minds and to no longer be conformed to this world. Then, we will be able to know Your will...Your good and perfect will.* We choose to do this as children of the most High King. We declare that we are each worshippers, and that is what we will spend our life doing and being. All that we know we are, we lay at Your feet. We put on the mantel of worshipping our King, for You alone are worthy to receive all the worship we have within us.

3. Lord, help us to let go of all the ways we've concocted to please You, but were neither in Your heart nor how You wanted to be worshipped during this time and season. We take off the old wine skin of worship and put on the new. We choose to love You with Heaven's love language and present ourselves to You in ways that please You. We adorn ourselves with what is pleasing in Your sight. We demand that our spirit-man within wake up and fully participate anew! We speak to our soul and flesh and forbid it to interfere with this undertaking.

4. We bow before You. We shout, sing, cry, dance, march, stand, yield to You and You alone. Whatever pleases You, King Jesus,

is what pleases us. We wave our flags before You; we paint our pictures; we sing prophetically—Heaven's songs; *we shout with the voice of triumph*; we even sing songs that may not be our genre, but are Yours. This releases the fragrance of Your presence that overwhelms us. The delight of You surpasses human understanding and words become inadequate to express what's within Your love-sick children who only have eyes for their beloved bridegroom.

5. If it were possible, we would write it in the sky for all to see and know. If it brought You more delight, we would shout it from the housetops. Our declaration of being a true worshipper begins with just a heart whisper, going into prayers spoken aloud, then to a low roar, turning into a tumultuous, uproarious sound that culminates in oblation to our King...*Emmanuel—God with us—* the shout of our hearts...the cry from within.

6. Let all who know our King cherish and obey You with obedience that is demonstrated in worship. Could it be that obedience is actually the highest form of worship? That is something we need to ponder. This one thought compels us to set our faces like flint: that we might worship You more and more each day, each hour, each moment we obey. Let the world be a witness to obedience that is radical, yet fills the longings of Your heart.

7. We move into dancing before You. We enter Your chamber to dance at Your feet. We grow weary in many ways, but this is not one of them. You deserve all the praise we can bring. You deserve all our adoration, for You are King of Kings and Lord of Lords. *What more can we give?* is our question. How can we model worship that causes even the angels to stop and take notice? We're not at that place yet. Once again we cry out "<u>Help</u>! Will You teach us? Will You show us? We are Your students!"

8. We long to present ourselves *as living sacrifices* because *that is our reasonable service.* Listen, to our cry: "Take us deeper... take us deeper in this thing called worship." Let us crown You with the loving kindness that You not only deserve, but our hearts overflow with to give You. Then and only then will we begin to experience the *height, depth, and width of Your love* towards us. How awesome this will be. How we linger just a little longer...one more moment...one more touch—that's what we want...just to be with You.

9. We do whatever it takes to be with Jesus...divine connection is what we desire. Could it be that His longing to be with us is even greater than ours? Now, we know that we know...we are supernatural beings locked temporarily in this natural body, not the opposite. What could be more wonderful than an encounter with the One for whom our hearts long for—brought on by the worship that You deserve? We now see Heaven coming to earth and earthly vessels encountering Heaven. All we can do is bow—breathing in and breathing out Your presence—with a heart that exudes thankfulness over and over and over again. All of this is for Your glory and in Jesus' name, Amen.

Prayer Seventeen:
Go Forth All Singers, Musicians,
Worshippers, and Intercessors

1. "It's time, Lord! Open our eyes; move us beyond our little caveat in our little world to Your possibilities…to Your potential. Release the hidden potential into reality. We say it is time for the musicians, singers, and intercessors to arise!" We trust You for Heavenly orchestration that plays out in day and night prayer. We are calling to those who have been called, disciplined, discipled, and destined to come before the King in worship and prayer. You said, *"My house shall be called a house of prayer."* Therefore we declare, **"Fill <u>the</u> Church; fill _____ (name Your church) with intercessors, Lord!"**

2. We call to the North, South, East, and West, "Intercessors and worshippers, come forth. That for which you were created is beckoning you." Do You feel it as You come and go? Do you sense it in the night watch? Do you see the fit? It's like a hand in a glove—exactly for what you were created. We declare, "Now is the time to say <u>yes</u> to Your heavenly Daddy. Now is the time to allow yourself to submit to the promotion to which God calls you."

3. *Promotion comes from the Lord.* You are making Your desires known to us. We hear You! The sounding of the call is loud. Heaven shouts, **"It's time! It's time! It's time! Release the singers; release the musicians; release the worshippers; release the intercessors**…all to their call…to their duty stations. Let the priests come forth; let the tribe of Judah arise in this hour to lead the people of God." That is Heaven's declaration. *Let those who have ears to hear, hear what the spirit of God is saying.* Let them take their stand to participate in their life calling and destiny.

4. We come into agreement with this, bringing Heaven to earth… bringing the supernatural into the natural realm. We do this today with our prayers and declarations. How can we do anything but come into agreement with our King? What is stopping us? Who is stopping us? In the mighty name of Jesus, we say "<u>NO!</u>— to every *power and principality in high places that have arrayed*

themselves against us!" We contend with these evil forces and shout with all our might, "You will <u>not</u> stop God's people! We release Your plans and purposes to come forth. We forbid anything less than Your perfect will and destiny to transpire."

5. Our prayer for this takes the form of a war cry from the warrior within. The angels are released and begin to set things in order. We don't hold back; we won't relent until the release has come full circle and the worshipping intercessors step up to the plate to pray and do what is in the heart of the Father for this generation. "Where can we go that You are not there? How can we escape You?" Even though that is our first thought, we know it was for this that we were created; therefore we forget trying to escape. Instead, we yield ourselves willingly to the call upon us for prayer and worship.

6. "But, we don't have time" is the whisper under our breath and also from those that feel the tugging and know the mandate. The spirit answers back, "Yes you do! Yes you do!" So, we pray wherever we are and whenever we can to fulfill this mandate—driving the car, cooking, cleaning, and working. We now understand it's everywhere…all the time! This is not only our lifestyle, but the lifestyle of the Bride—the Church.

7. So, we release prayers today that "many will begin anew, picking up this call, including those who have let go of this desire for whatever reason, and especially ones who have been set apart *since before creation* for this." We declare, "**Let the set apart ones come forth. *Stop kicking against the goads.*** Get in God's presence, <u>pray</u> His will, <u>sing</u> His song, <u>release</u> deliverance over His people—over the world." We say "align yourself with God for it is a NOW time and a NOW season."

8. Who can flee Your presence? Wherever we go, You are there. We cannot resist that for which we were created! Only we can make that choice for ourselves. But, we say to all, "<u>Listen</u> …for the Father is calling; <u>listen</u>… for the time of release is now; <u>listen</u>… for we know You are establishing Your will on the earth." Today, we're praying and releasing the ability to hear clearly. The word we're releasing is **<u>clarity</u>**. Let clarity come forth for the people of God.

9. The question is this, "Who will participate? Who will involve themselves with the *bread of life* and the *light of the world*? Who will be bread or light to another?" It is as simple as "yes"

g to be willing." We release strength, power,
e who are hedging <u>and</u> over those that have
ry is, "God, use all the worshipping warriors
ors for Your good will and pleasure."

Heaven's perfect will to come to earth through prayers,
gs, and declarations. Take us to the next level. Teach us
supernaturally. Let us progress beyond our years...not only in
singing abilities and excellence with our instruments, but also
in our prayers and songs that come forth. Let Heaven invade
us in our sleep, on the way to work, in the kitchen, while the
lawn is being mowed.... LET THE INVASION BEGIN! Fill our
church and this area with intercessors. We declare that "Your
house shall be *a house of prayer* for *Your glory* and *Your name's
sake.*"

11. Come closer than we've ever thought possible. Let us feel
    Your touch—Your breath. We want to know You! Wrap Your
    love around us as a garland around our neck. Let us know how
    pleased You are with us by our simple, "Yes; we're willing to be
    willing." Do not allow the enemy to stop us or defile us. We say,
    "**<u>No to the forces of evil</u>**; You can't have the singing psalmists,
    the mighty intercessors, or the worshipping warriors!"

12. Lord, teach us how to offer worship and prayer that is pure and
    undefiled. Let us *never grow weary* in doing Your will. As a
    matter of fact, let this be *strength to our bodies and marrow to
    our bones.* Help us be equippers of the saints and leaders of the
    pack. You are God and there is none like You. Let us understand
    this statement and live it out with everything we say, sing, pray,
    and do. May You receive all the glory, honor, and praise <u>for this</u>
    in Jesus' name, Amen!

Prayer Eighteen:
Heavenly Prayers for the Dying, Afflicted, Hurting, and Their Healthcare Workers

1. Father, we pray, "Do not let this one fact escape us: *to You a day is as a thousand years and a thousand years are as a day. You are not slow in keeping Your promises as some understand slowness.* So we declare, "*Your will be done on earth as it is in Heaven.* Let the will of God manifest before our eyes." As this happens, we become more and more thankful that You are *patient, not wanting anyone to perish but all to come to repentance.*

2. We also declare, *"It is the mercy of God that leads to repentance."* So today, we proclaim, **"mercy"** and we also thank You for Your kindness towards us—sinners and for all sinners. We know *that all have sinned and fallen short of the glory of God.* Daily, we're led to repent for sins of commission and omission—things we've knowingly done and things that we're oblivious to doing. Lord, don't let our emotions get the best of us and carry us away to continue in this thing called sin. Don't allow the world to shape us and be swept away to worldly places forsaking the rich heritage we have in You.

3. Today, we're crying out for our family, our church, this area and this nation. Lord, there are so many hurting people who need Your attention and help. Hospitals, medical centers of varying kinds, hospices, nursing homes, and rehabilitation centers all testify to this. As people stream in and out, not understanding that *You sent Your Word to heal and by Your stripes we're healed,* we take this time to call out to You not only for the sick and dying, but for all who take care of Your precious cargo. It can be such a painful and thankless job at times. Other times, the invasion of Your presence is obvious to all and then thanksgiving goes out.

4. Lord, help Your doctors, nurses, and other medical professionals that give of themselves sacrificially to love on Your people. To some it's only a job, but to others, it's the God of the Universe breathing life-giving words and encouragement to each patient. It is also the extension of Your hands reaching through these

'sionals to people in pain, afflicted by
٦ myriad of other physical and emotional
٬٫e often attributed to spiritual roots that
٫alt with and/or the outcome of living in a fallen
٫i so, we declare, "You are in love with these hurting
. You shed Your blood for them on the cross." When You
٫٫d, *"It is finished,"* You were including these—the hurting,
dying, afflicted, and lost. Father, let the health care workers
not lose sight of the way You use them for good to help save
lives. We emphatically state, "These lives are intended for good
to accomplish what is now being done—the saving of many
lives. *"*

5. So today, the prayers that we shout from the housetops are for
   all who are infirmed or involved in their caretaking. Would You
   send intercessors to stand in the gap to pray prayers that initiate
   healing? Would You help us lay hands on them and see them
   recover? Would You allow Heaven to come down and heal these
   people? Hear our cries for Your people to come forth and see the
   multitude of needs in this area. Open our eyes, Lord! Let Your
   people establish prayers for the doctors, nurses, families, and
   other workers. Send relief.

6. We stand united to proclaim that the enemy—sickness, infirmity,
   pain, and disease—is bound, in the name of Jesus. These things
   must bow to Your name and the Word of God—*by Your stripes,
   healing comes.* We appropriate the finished work of the cross to
   go forth. We take the position of watchman on the wall, knowing
   that our position in Christ is that *we're seated far above all
   principalities and powers.*

7. We continually give thanks to the King of Kings and Lord of
   Lords for the magnificence of Your creation. Your mysteries
   become obvious as they are unlocked to those who study the
   human body. You give answers to Your workers that are too
   incredible for words. We thank You for diagnoses that come in
   the form of heavenly blue-prints, released because of the cries
   and tears of Your saints. Once again, You are too amazing for
   words. So, we bow down and worship You even more.

8. Our prayer is also for the families who make the daily trek back
   and forth to hospitals and other places of rehabilitation to help
   the sick and bless the dying. "God, give strength; send anointing;
   release encouraging words; allow peace to overwhelm each and

every situation. *Allow the peace that passes all understanding to engulf and overtake every person and every situation.* Send wisdom, knowledge, heavenly information and revelation to all involved, so that correct and godly decisions come forth. We plead the blood of Jesus in these situations and continue to thank You for Your help." At the same time, we recognize our humanity, along with our frailties. We ask, *"What is it that causes You to be mindful of us? Who can know Your ways?"* We say, "We can!" That brings us full-circle once again to declare, "How awesome You are!" (SELAH)

9. Father, we need the ability to value LIFE—the same value You place on it. Give us heavenly prayers for the dying, afflicted, and hurting—prayers that not only delight Your heart, but bring tangible peace and Your presence to every situation, especially those described as *sickness unto death.* Teach us also how to pray prayers that initiate the ministry You have for every situation. We stand in need of Your help.

10. Help us to know when to call on the elders of the church. You said, *"The prayers of the righteous avail much."* Let our prayers do more than just avail...let them prevail until the greater work—the finished work of the cross is manifested. Teach the recipients of these prayers how to receive the finished work of the cross! Lord, we don't know how to pray, unless You teach us; they don't know how to receive unless You teach them. What a quandary this is...yet, we trust You.

11. You hold all the answers in Your hand. *Just one touch of Your garment* and we are healed. You did it then; do it now; do it today. Let us operate as an extension of Your hands. Use us in signs, wonders, miracles, faith, and healings. You are the great physician. Let us participate in that facet of who You are, that all may know and give You glory.

12. Father, we've grown weary. Help us in our weariness; we've given up too soon. Give us the ability to keep on keeping on—even when the doctors give no hope. Lord, You know that *without hope, the heart grows sick.* Send us light at the end of the tunnel. Be strong in us and through us. Lord, as we sit and sit, wait and wait, we're asking You to pour out Your grace so that we can endure this process. **"We are tired; we are weary".** But, You never grow tired or weary. Hear our petitions this day; hear our requests. Help us to tap into Your limitless strength and

apprehend that which You apprehended for us on the cross. We don't think we will make it otherwise. When will this end? At the same time, we look for a reprieve, we don't stop fighting. We release peace and Your will...continuing to fight against death and forbid it to overtake these situations even one day before God's appointed time. We are Your children...hear us today, we pray! Give us grace and relief...Your perfect will be done...not our will but thy will in Jesus' name, Amen!

Prayer Nineteen:
Caretakers of God's Children—
Including the "Throw Away" Kids

1. "This generation...this present generation...their parents and grandparents...those taking care of Your kids...even the ones in foster care and orphanages!" That's what's on Your heart Lord! You are so great and greatly to be praised. Your ways and thoughts are so much higher than ours. Everything You establish is for Your good pleasure and the welfare of a nation. You will not let go until You see the work You've begun completed with fruit for all to *taste and see that the Lord is good.* Thanks for not giving up on us, Your children. Thanks for placing us in a family and loving on us through imperfect people with whom we can grow and be established. Lord, we praise You for being a *father to the fatherless and a defender of widows.* You found it good to set Your people in families. You don't want Your people to be alone.

2. The attack on the family is so great. Parents seem to be at wits-end trying just to survive, much less flourish. Lord, do not let parents, grandparents, or foster parents *grow weary in well doing*; but would You remind them to *acknowledge You in all their ways and then You would direct their paths*? You say, *"How good and how pleasant it is for brothers to dwell together in unity."* We're praying today, "Let it begin in homes...in our homes...with us. Then let it spread to all whom we know and to all whom come in contact with us. Don't stop until it travels this entire country." We are talking about a nation that has its firm foundation and strong convictions based in the Word of God and established on sound biblical principles.

3. We are crying out for parents and grandparents everywhere. Help women to be in tune with their children. Release mothering skills that help mothers walk in wisdom, undistracted by the tug of the world. Send anointing to aid all who are mothering children—biological mothers, grandmothers, foster and adoptive mothers—so all feel well equipped for the task at hand. Anoint each one with Heavenly information—words of wisdom and knowledge to accomplish what is on the heart of

the Father for every child. Place the word of God at the center of their lives; give each one stamina and determination to go forward with what is right, even though it may be unpopular or not the latest fad.

4. Release parents to much prayer and fasting. Let the lasting fruit from this come forth and the difference be obvious to all. Discharge unity between husbands, wives, moms and dads on how to accomplish this. We release the ability to discipline and raise children in a manner that pleases the King of Kings. Do not allow the enemy to pit one parent against the other. Allow the practical things that every person needs to function in life prevail and be part of the foundational training kids receive at home. **Help all parents Lord! All need Your help!** Train us, so that in the midst of a busy life we don't forget to teach and establish the things that are most important—the things on Your heart.

5. Grant dads the supernatural courage to be very involved in the lives of their children and to lead with love, not harshness. Allow this love to play out in holiness and righteousness that gains him respect from every family member. Let dads *taste and see that the Lord is good.* From this abundance, let dads impart godly fear that produces righteous fruit that leads to holy deeds that end up in godly lifestyles for the entire family. Top that with the ability to communicate and walk in sacrificial love that is unconditional and forthright—a pleasing aroma to the Lord.

6. Allow dads to walk in a supernatural dimension of fatherhood that demonstrates tangible love to the mother of their kids. Give strong backbones and courageous actions that send the message of unconditional love that translates to children, "Have no fear; *as much as depends upon me, I will live at peace with all;* I will never divorce Mom!" Let this fact be so settled that the "D" word is not a part of their vocabularies. Release respect for dads throughout the entire family and allow moms to model this at all times.

7. Lord, there are people who have grown up on their own... not much input, love, or devotion from parents. Some have experienced abuse of many kinds and most of it is hidden and goes undetected. These children have become, for lack of a better term, the 'throw away' kids. How can anyone exploit, mistreat and ignore these beautiful treasures created in Your image? The hurt and pain from this settles in hearts, making it difficult

for those damaged to give and receive love. It can be next to impossible for them to think of themselves the way You do and understand their heavenly Daddy is crazy about them.

8. So today, we cry out for these 'throw away' kids who are on Your heart. *Though a father and mother forsake their child, You never will.* We trust You to break the cycle and reveal truth. We pray for friends, relatives, teachers, and others to take bold stands that will uncover abuse so that help may be obtained. Now is the time for Heaven to come down and release the *healing balm of Gilead* that will break through to hurting, neglected, and abused people who have been tormented by broken hearts. We *stand in the gap to make up the hedge* and forgive parents who would do such a thing. Then, we cry out as Jesus did on the cross, *"Forgive them; they know not what they do."*

9. Father, how long can this go on? How long can these people survive in this state? We're crying "Adoption" for those in orphanages and without parents. Mold hearts that will rescue children who need parents. Our prayers are for these hurting, lonely people who may not survive unless You intervene. We're praying that their wounds would be healed and their harsh memories be eradicated by the Father's touch. We're saying, "Let Your love for people transcend every circumstance and settle on these children, teenagers, young adults, adults, and elderly people. Take away the internal scars they are carrying because of rejection and abuse as children. Mend the hearts of the hurting. Allow the finger of God to touch the deepest, darkest places and let the light of Your presence flood in."

10. We declare, "It is time for the enemy to be defeated and the Most High God to come forth in triumph. Let this success shine forth for all to see. No more defeat." God has set people in a family for a reason and a purpose. Let the reasons and purposes come forth. We decree it is a time of destiny. Let destinies be revealed. Let God's purposes for individual lives come forth. It is for this reason that this prayer is prayed. Our goal is to establish on earth the will of Heaven. Use men and women who understand and have Your heart in this matter to take up the mantel of parenting to fulfill this. Help is needed to walk in this sacrificial love. This is where the rubber meets the road in this thing called Christianity.

11. It's for the kid's sake and God's name sake. Release help in a timely manner, that *none would be lost*. Come forth and release the providential grace required in this hour for Your children and their parents. Release godly heritage. Teach parents, grandparents, foster and adoptive parents how to receive and appropriate **all** that Your blood purchased on the cross. HELP! Help is needed, Lord! This is a difficult task. The future of this generation and this godly nation is at stake. We yield to You and thank You for what is transpiring right now as we pray because our God is alive. You hear and answer the prayers of the saints. Thanks be to God…all glory and honor and praise go out to the King of Kings and the Lord of Lords. For it's in Jesus' name we pray this, Amen and Amen!

Prayer Twenty:
A Prayer for the Nation

1. *Righteousness exalts a nation, but sin is a disgrace to any people.* "Wake up, people! Wake up and take a righteous stand is our cry. Father, forgive this nation! Does this country really know the consequences of its actions?" So, we admonish all to pray; cry out; seek God to remove the stench that comes from sin. Lord, remove the disgrace that many have brought upon families, churches, this area, and this nation. Annihilate false doctrines and the extinction of divine truth.

2. Who can stand in the midst of a sovereign God and not feel remorse? Where is the godly sorrow that brings repentance? Lord, we release *sorrow that produces* in Your people not only *earnestness, indignation* and *alarm;* but also a *longing,* and a *concern* for the things that grieve You. Grant this to play out in a *readiness to see justice done* in our nation with our politicians— from the lowest level to the highest, including the judicial system and all judges.

3. Let the judges corporately report, "We have done all that we know to do in our own lives in taking a stand against idolatry, injustice, and unrighteousness. We are carrying out the goals of the constitution in the spirit set forth by our forefathers. Our aspiration is to *prove ourselves innocent* of sin and to carry out God's mandate to the best of our abilities. We have *humbled ourselves, prayed, sought God, and turned from our* wicked ways. We do this so that You, Almighty God, *would hear from Heaven and come and heal our land.*"

4. We declare to the land of this nation, "Be healed, in the name of Jesus. Be what God has intended you to be. Do not back down from being *dedicated to the proposition that not only are all men created equal but are also endowed by their Creator with certain inalienable rights...with life, liberty, and the pursuit of happiness* as core values. This includes the unborn, sick, and elderly. Allow freedom to ring once again so that all may know You are God and there is none like You. We declare freedom in our lives, families and churches. Let the people of God rise up today and pray the heart of the father for this nation."

5. *Who can lift up their eyes* to idols and continue the same path when Jehovah God is so in love with us, His creation, and has released blessing in so many ways? Just as *in the days of Noah,* people continue with abandonment and do not seem to take notice of the days, times, or season. Let us be retrospective in our observations and not abandon truth. Our cry is for people to come forth who *will humble themselves and pray* so that this nation can stand and the kingdom of God advance amidst turmoil, strife, and upheaval. Where are the tears and prayers for You to collect in Your heavenly bowls that many have poured out, not relenting until You are preeminent over every area of our lives and this country?

6. We pray, "Release once again the godly heritage that this nation was founded upon. Let that which this country was predestined to be come forth." Let Christians once again vote in godly men and women who are not ashamed of the gospel and allow the Spirit of the living God to bring forth heavenly plans for this nation. We bow to the orchestration of our King!

7. Allow our vote to reflect a people whose hearts are lined up with God. Let us once again vote in people that will work tirelessly to bring about what is best for this country, not what is best for them personally. Remove the greedy and those that are power-hungry. Bring forth servant leadership of the people, for the people, and by the people. Let hearts that are aligned with this statement, "Ask not what Your country can do for You; but what You can do for Your country," be at the forefront of all who run for office—giving freely of their time, money, and life with no expectation of earthly gain.

8. *Can a nation be saved in a day*? We say, "Yes! Let it be so!"We come into agreement with God today and pray for the political structure to align with righteousness and holiness. We cry out that those in office **that will not do the will of God** be removed. Jehovah Jireh, our provider, come forth! Jehovah Shalom, release this country to peace once again...fear must go.

9. We know that the *heart of the king is in the hand of God and that He directs it like a watercourse.* We stand in agreement with You on this and shout, "Direct, direct, direct! Holy orchestration is our cry! Do not allow the rich heritage and providential foundation laid by our forefathers to be uprooted by the wiles of the devil, worked out through evil men and women whose hearts

are hardened to the things of God. Lord, if they will not be saved and follow You, let people come forth who will no longer tolerate this and vote them out of office. Permit their replacements to be hand-picked by Heaven."

10. Do not let the people of God shrink back while the forces of evil rise up to overtake this nation. We stand in the gap and release prayers that will get Your attention. We release the groaning from within that will reverberate in Heaven. This releases prayers without words that releases anointing that breaks the yoke. We stand unafraid and unabashed to state, "This is one nation under God, and we will not tolerate anything less."

11. Therefore, the political structure and politicians must bow to Almighty God. Your arm is not too short. You will <u>not</u> tolerate Your godly foundation and structure to be torn down. God will <u>not</u> bow to man; rather, man will bow to the only one who *is able to save to the uttermost*. Then, we will see the people of God rise up and champion the cause of Christ once again.

12. So, today, in the midst of what appears to be sin and defeat, we shout, "**God is able!** You <u>will</u> do the things You said You will do. You are more than able to raise up Your army in these last days to go forth in victory." (The Bride is listening.) We are putting on our combat boots and standing at attention, ready to do Your bidding. We repent for our sins, the sins of this nation and those in public office that have steered the inhabitants the wrong way! Forgive all; come and heal our land once again. We pray this in the name of Jesus Christ our Lord and Savior, Amen!

Prayer Twenty One:
For the Entertainment Industry and Media

1. Blow the trumpet in Zion. Sound the alarm. Release the angelic host to come to heal and come and to do God's bidding by removing the tares and showing up with God's presence. We declare, "Release, release, release…Let the Heavens be opened with angels ascending and descending today for the glory of God. We release miracles, signs, and wonders to accomplish Your will. Let the people of God arise in faith today to receive all You have for them. We come into agreement with God and declare Your will be done on earth <u>today</u> at _____ (name your church) as it is in Heaven for Your glory, in Jesus' name!"

2. We admonish, "It's <u>not</u> time to stand idly by and allow the devil to beat up on the people of God any longer. It is time to get Your attention and allow Your presence to make the necessary adjustments". We want what's on Your heart to overwhelm and overtake this human flesh that desires to take the path of least resistance. Who can know God's mind and plans? Your friends and the prophets can and do. We position ourselves prophetically as your friend, seeing and hearing. All that does not line up with You must step aside. When that happens, Heavenly gates open, and the King of Glory comes in.

3. *Who is this King of Glory*? You are the one who is *mighty in battle*. You are the friend to the friendless, a father to those without fathers and a spouse to the unmarried. You are everything to all of us. You keep us in the palm of Your hands and *under the shadow of Your wings*. You breathe and allow Your breath to cover us. Your joy for all Your kids springs forth when we least expect it. You are holy and wholly to be praised. May You receive all the praise and adoration that is within us, and may we give it freely to You for You alone are worthy!

4. When we look and see *how the wicked have prospered*, our hearts sink. But, then, we *realize the end of the matter* and the end of their story. So, we grieve for them and our tears reach Heaven. You are as much in love with them as You are with us. We hearken to hear Your words. With all that we are, we try to fulfill what pleases You to the best of our abilities. We

yield ourselves to Your compassion and Your love. Being full of God, we have You to give away to the hurting and dying. We see the devastation of the people and cry out, "Help!"

5. At the bottom of this destruction, we take notice that the entertainment industry has penetrated into all areas of life. We cry out for righteousness to have its way once again in the midst of a dark and dying world: *Your will be done; Your kingdom come...* Our cry to the Most High is, "Don't allow the imaginations of the dark places of the mind to be the norm for what entertains. Once again let us return to virtuous, respectable, and decent living. Let us make productions that glorify You, O Lord, and uplift the human soul."

6. We cry out for the people that <u>write</u>, <u>direct</u>, <u>produce</u>, and participate in any way in the things that come from the entertainment business, also including all arts and sporting events. We declare, "Lord, come and have Your way! Come and breathe upon this group. May their gifts and talents be used for *Your* glory and not the enemies. Come and allow Your presence to overwhelm and save. We release salvation to the entertainment industry."

7. "Don't allow money to be the god that rules here any longer." We know *that the love of money is the root of all evil.* Release that false idolatrous love from this industry. Free the unsaved to receive Christ and escape the miry pit that holds them captive. Let the people of God rise up and cry out for these people that are successful in the world's eyes, but are so empty and are unaware of their emptiness. Fill each to overflowing with Your love. Give anointing that produces books, movies, TV shows, and radio programs that encourage hurting people instead of adding to their disillusionment and misery.

8. Abba Father Daddy, protect the Christians who work in these fields. Guard their hearts and minds. Allow their voices and opinions to be filled with love and compassion. Release righteous words that will penetrate to people at the highest level with authority that can and will make changes for the good. Give Your children wisdom, grace, and peace as they traverse this mine field.

9. Use the saved and unsaved to advance Your Kingdom and uphold Your will. Invade in such a way that Your agenda is advanced without their realization. Stop the forces of evil that

have aligned themselves and do the bidding of Satan. Annihilate all the politically correct agendas that nauseate Your heart and are a stench to this land selling the souls of humanity into darkness. This money-driven way of life fueled by fear and its forces must stop. All must bow to the name of Jesus.

10. We say today that all entertainment, arts, and sporting events must bow to the King of Kings and Lord of Lords. None will stop His Kingdom from advancing and His second coming. We say the homosexual agenda, the abortion industry, perversion, pornography, child abuse and all addictions must bow to the name that's above ever other name—JESUS! Depicting Christianity in a negative light must cease. All the sleaze that goes against You and your word must yield. All media of any kind, including the news media, must bow to the name of Jesus.

11. We release people to come alongside the Most High God and produce manuscripts, news shows, books, movies, programs, music videos, magazines, newspapers, internet sites, musical events, shows, and more that will overtake the demonic culture of this nation and release media that will promote and bless this country once again. We say, "Creativity, come forth. Supernatural wisdom and anointing, be released. Writers that have been ordained and destined for the glory of God be established. Godly editors, arise. Actors, cameramen, producers, executive producers of all kinds, etc., come to the righteous calling that You have for each. Answer God's call and bidding. Let it begin today!"

12. Rejoice and be glad, for the God of the universe is calling. Step up to the plate and take your rightful place. It is time for all media to once again be released to the light. Darkness must flee. We are praying, seeking, calling out, crying, decreeing, and declaring that *Jesus is Lord* over all media, entertainment, arts, and sports—including Nashville, Hollywood, and Las Vegas. This includes the music industry, books, magazine, newspapers, the Internet, cell phones and radio also.

13. We speak to the airwaves and release the name of *Jesus and the finished work of the cross.* We declare, "Yield righteousness, leading to holiness. Let today be the day when darkness flees and even the airways display Your glory." Father, we stand in agreement with You and *call things that are not as though they*

186

are. Today is the day *that every knee bows and every tongue confesses* in the entertainment industry that *Jesus is Lord.*" The shift comes and it is felt by the world. Thanks be to God and all praise goes to You forever and ever, Amen!

Prayer Twenty Two:
For Ministers and a Call to the Wall

1. Lord, we know that we know that we know that we know that prayer changes things. So today, we cry out that You would bless and encourage all involved in ministry and especially the five-fold. *Far be it from us that we should sin against* You, Almighty God, *by failing to pray* for those who are helping the people on Your heart. We call out to You today, *lifting holy hands without wrath or doubting,* for the apostles, prophets, evangelists, pastors, teachers, missionaries, and all involved in ministry and their families.

2. Let appreciation be at the forefront of Your people's minds for those who have sold-out their lives to advance the Kingdom of God and see many souls saved. We declare, "Let the praises of God be on our lips for the men and women who have answered You daily to sacrifice their lives to flow in the river of God's calling and anointing. Let many testify that You are awesome and because of You, Your ministers and fellow workers are anointed and blessed."

3. Father, our hearts remains heavy as we ponder those who have become discouraged and have laid their calling down for whatever reasons. For some, the attack of the enemy has become too great. For others, the price was higher than anticipated. So today, we release fresh grace over them and call them to pick it back up and begin anew. We release fresh anointing for the situations at hand. We're praying for people to come back to their lives' calling once again. Enter in…the Father is calling.

4. Lord, release the five-fold ministers and their ministry to Your churches. Let joy overflow by having all that is needed in each church to do the *work at hand.* Let this motto ring out, *"We will follow the five-fold ministers as they follow the Lord."* Do not let Your ministers and preachers of the gospel *grow weary in well doing. Let them acknowledge You in all their ways,* so that their paths are directed by You from Heaven.

5. Lord, we have seen the *beauty of Your holiness* and have tasted from the waters of Life. To the extent of our Biblical knowledge, training, and experience, we understand the powers within. Yet, we are well aware of the schemes the enemy has set against

ministers and their families. Father, <u>give</u> courage, <u>build</u> strength, and <u>release</u> the anointing to establish Biblical strongholds for God in the places of their calling and planting. Give abilities beyond their years and grace that extends them into the places You want them to go. Give words that, when spoken, have the power to establish what is on the heart of the Father. Holy Spirit, teach all to be grace-filled and able to freely give 1 Cor. 13 love to all.

6. Many times we have experienced the glory of Your power present in Your ministers. We have also seen You transform their weaknesses into strengths, establishing them as a light in the earth. When others have only seen a shepherd boy, You often see a king. A man after Your heart, David, is a good example. It's the same today. The weak and undesirable parts of the body are transformed with just one touch from the Master's hand. Impossible situations...but God...Release over and over again the "<u>but Gods</u>" and the "<u>suddenlies</u>" that all may stand in awe of You, my King!

7. Discharge such godly character and self control that the enemy is unable to touch Your hand picked five-fold ministers; all accusations against them come to naught. Stop the enemy in his tracks before the assignments are released; send divine, angelic protection to battle and thwart the devil's plans in the heavenly realm.

8. Father, we confess there are weaknesses. Therefore we take up the mantel to stand in the gap, even when we don't know how to pray, we *allow the Spirit to search our hearts and intercede through us with groans that words cannot express.* We allow the Spirit to intercede for ministers in accordance with God's will. We do that today. We're seeking You on their behalf. We're releasing heavenly visitations that bring open Heavens to congregations and surrounding areas.

9. Through this declaration, we also aim to restore biblical preaching that may not be politically correct but will capture the hearts and minds of Your people, thus, changing nations. We are releasing ministers to walk in fearlessness in the face of adversity. We are anointing voices to be released in the pulpit—voices that will declare throne-room, Biblical truth, even when it appears to be political suicide to do so. We are praying that churches everywhere will be established with *all* five of the five-fold

ministries and workers will be fully trained to handle all that lies ahead.

10. God, the church must have Your ordained, established government yielded to Your way of doing things. Without it, the advancement of the Kingdom may be paralyzed and unable to go forward in these days and times. This is a critical time in the history of our nation and the world. HELP!

11. We desperately desire for You to release Your glory over all five-fold ministers and the Church. We declare over and over, "*Open up ye gates that the King of Glory may come in.*" You enter through gates that can only be established through much worship and intercession. We're calling the Church *to the wall* to pray. Forgive Your people for prayerlessness. God, use our prayers and those of the faithful to build the walls that will establish the gates that will usher you through. We stand to seek you on the wall. Enjoin others to this cause, we pray.

12. Jesus, as You sit at the right hand of the Father, could we intercede with You on this topic? Would You give us words to pray this into existence? Would You bring Heaven to earth at just the right time and establish this at _____ (name your church) and all God-ordained churches? We are crying out for You to establish Your heart in Your Church—the body at large. Bring forth the *apostles, prophets, evangelists, pastors, and teachers to equip Your Church to do the work of the ministry* in our day…in our time…for our good…but ultimately for Your glory. Thank You for hearing our cry in Jesus' name, Amen.

Prayer Twenty Three:
For the Persecuted Church

1. *The Lord is our portion.* There is no other and none like You. The extent of our inheritance lies in this statement. You are our all in all. You are everything to us. *As the deer pants for the water, so my soul pants for You.* As surely as You live, so do we.
2. Every breath we breathe, Lord, is for You alone. We want to be a reflection of Your glory—the essence of who You are to all whom we encounter. **The shout of the King is within us.** All that we need is found securely in You. That fact is overwhelming to us.
3. We drink in Your presence. This pleasure overwhelms us and brings us to tears. Could You, the God of the Universe really be madly in love with us—even more than we are with You... more than we love our own children? How is that possible? We can't comprehend it. Yet, we soak it in, receive it, and dwell on that one thought until we can handle it no more. We are forever ruined.
4. Our thoughts and focus are on You and You alone. Who can know You, my King? We can. Thank You for the revelations that You constantly give so that we can personally know You. You take our breath away. As we breathe You in, a satisfaction that reaches to the depths of our being overtakes us. We can barely move; we can barely continue our activity. (SELAH)
5. "Presence of God, power of God, anointing of God...FALL! Presence of God, power of God, anointing of God...FALL! Fill us up to overflowing. Overflow through us to all whom we meet," is our prayer. We pursue only You; then we're filled as Your presence encapsulates us. Next we're poured out. (It looks like us, but, all we have to offer of any value is YOU. So we pour out YOU over and over and over again.) The cycle repeats: We're refilled once again. "Presence of God, power of God, anointing of God...FALL! Presence of God, power of God, anointing of God...FALL!" That brings the shift. We feel it. We sense it. We see it.
6. What is it that You require of us? Is it *to do justice?* Is it *to love mercy?* Is it *to walk humbly with our God?* We say "YES" to all three and make it our life's goal and ambition to please You in

191

all things! There is nowhere to flee from Your presence. You are with us wherever we go. Your grace overwhelms every situation and, with just one glance, overtakes all enemies.

7. Thank You, Lord, for this divine presence. It is available for every situation and every follower of Christ. We pour it out today in prayer for the persecuted church. It is difficult for our minds to comprehend the hatred that the enemy purports on Your people in other nations. We plead for those who have lost family members because they have stood up for their faith. We cry out for those in prison to have the courage to continue on and to **never** reject Jesus. We implore You for those who, in standing up for Christianity, have lost everything and every person who can be named as family. We beg for children who are parent-less because parents have chosen to stand for Jesus and not deny their faith. *Thank You that You are a father to the fatherless, a defender of widows, that You set the lonely in families and lead forth prisoners with singing.*

8. Lord, pour out anointing and grace for the young and old to continue, even as *darkness—yea deep darkness—covers the earth.* Provide for the persecuted church in every nation in ways that are limitless. Give courage not only to continue standing, but in the midst of persecution to be a witness. Let requests go forward that move the heart of Abba Father Daddy that is seen in tangible ways.

9. May cries reach to Heaven for each persecuted people group and release all to be saved. Make available the words, timing, anointing, and miracles that will change families, towns, cities, and nations. **O God, strength from on High is needed**. Grant eyes to see what the spirit of God is doing and fortitude to do it. Bequeath insight as to how to pray for those who oppress, murder, and persecute. Give Your servants grace to love and to forgive their enemies. We stand in the gap today, forgiving and repenting on their behalf. May the glory of Your presence on Christian faces cause those persecuting to fall to their knees in repentance, come to salvation and be set free from their own chains and bondage...for You died for them, also. Thank You for the sufficiency of Your blood.

10. Father, many suffer in their physical bodies because of the beatings and torture. We plead with You, "Grant grace, not only

to endure, but to *rejoice that they participate in the sufferings of Christ, so that they may be overjoyed when Your glory is revealed.* Miraculously take away pain and agony. Send medical help in a timely manner. Provide ministering and healing angels to be released to those who are suffering. Award faith that supersedes all encounters from the enemy. Furnish plans and strategies that will grow the church in spite of all that is taking place. Ordain pastors, missionaries, and leaders who will carry out Heavenly plans and Biblical mandates that fulfill God-given responsibilities."

11. Father, these are Your children. We cry, "Send what is needed for them at the time that it is needed. Give steadfast hearts that continue in the midst of persecution and difficult situations. Hear our cry; hear our plea. Send help, O Lord!" The blood of the saints and of the martyrs call out to You today. Release the breaker anointing; *open up ye gates and let the King of Glory in.* All of this and more we pray in Jesus' mighty name, Amen!

Prayer Twenty Four:
Those in Desert Experiences

1. Lord, we're crying out for those who are in a desert season of their lives. Jesus, as You were led into the desert for forty days, praying and fasting, we understand that You are drawing some into the desert; others have gone there of their own volition. Some have followed the devil—unaware that it was him and the schemes he has planned. So today, we lift them up and cry out that You would be with them during this time and open their eyes to see, know, and experience truth.

2. Father, many are looking for a mountaintop experience with You and instead are feeling alone and shut out as the desert experience has become overwhelming. During this time, be ever so close to Your kids. Allow this desert experience to bring an intimacy that is so close and personal that You manifest how *You stick closer than a brother* at all times.

3. Take everything that began as a negative and *work it together for good*. Lord, release the miraculous power that only comes from an encounter with You. Allow those wandering to accomplish what is on Your heart and to roam no more. For those who are experiencing this due to wrong choices and wrong decisions, forgive them. Allow them to learn quickly from their mistakes and continue on to accomplish the destiny You have for them. For those who have followed Satan into the desert, give time and space for reexamination of their lives, followed quickly by repentance and rededication to follow You.

4. For those whom You have drawn away by the Holy Spirit *to be conformed to the image of Christ*, use this time to have its perfect work accomplished. Permit growth and commitment to the Lord to be at the forefront of all that transpires. Allow anointing and grace to be a garland around their necks, with only the burdens of the Lord placed on their backs. Every other burden must yield to the Lord and be removed at this time.

5. Father, some of Your children suffer from unbiblical compromise and political correctness that come from divided hearts—*tossed to and fro by every wind of doctrine*. **This is not Your plan**. Align each one in Your perfect will and way. Forsake not and allow every wandering to be short—only long enough to accomplish

Your will in each life. Help each one relinquish all they are to You and Your ways during this time. Tolerate nothing to be held back from the love of our Daddy.

6. Lord, help us! Help all of us differentiate between the desert experience where we are tempted by the enemy and tested *to see if we be in the faith—and* lead us to the top of the mountain by going through the valley first. The valley teaches and trains mountaintop survival skills. Without these, our destiny may be delayed. For we know that *without holiness no one will see God.*

7. It is in the valley times of our lives that You train us to be in Your presence. It is during these seasons that the Spirit of God strips away all things that do not *pertain to life and godliness.* It is here that we learn to yield all of ourselves for total cleaning, so that we can truly *present ourselves as a living sacrifice.*

8. Once again, we wonder who can really know the mind of Christ. Again, we know the answer is US! We can, because You reveal Yourself to us over and over again as we travel through the valleys of our lives. You reveal the love that can only be experienced and known during these times. How wonderful Your ways are toward us as we travel through the valleys and the deserts in this season.

9. Without these times, could we really understand and experience the mountain top to the fullest extent possible? Could we transcend to the highest of heights? Could the depth of God really be breathed into our innermost being? O God, Your ways are too wonderful for words. We stand in amazement of You again and again. How we love You Lord.

10. Thank You for growing us up in You as we travel through the valleys on our way to the mountaintop experiences our hearts longs for. Forgive us for not understanding or appreciating all that You're doing there. Thank You for purifying our hearts so that we *can see You.* We do long to partake of the blessings we receive because we know *the pure in heart will see God.* What more can we ask? Once again, as we ponder this, we are at a loss for words. We dwell on it a little longer and thank You over and over for all the work You're doing in us. It's in Jesus' precious name that we pray all of this, Amen.

Prayer Twenty Five:
Family, Friends, Freedom and Faith

1. Father, when we gaze and meditate upon the Trinity, the thankfulness that is on the tip of our tongues explodes forth from each of us. We wrestle with finding adequate words for this task before us. What can compare to our God? Nothing! Whose love deeply touches the recesses of our hearts in a way that no other can? Only Yours. So today, we adore You with our prayers, asking that You would bring forth from us praise and adoration that is worthy of a King—especially the King of Kings and the Lord of Lords.

2. We hold nothing back and release all that we are to this daunting task. Fill our hearts with the attitude of gratitude that would send forth *a sweet fragrance to Your nostrils*. Permit this praise to be our *reasonable service*. Allow every thought and every fiber of our being to resonate with praise to the Father, Son, and Holy Spirit. Let Your *name be lifted high* that all may give You praise, worship, and adoration, allowing You to gain the fame that You alone are worthy to receive.

3. We give you thanks and praise for family, friends, freedom, and faith. Lord, we know that we have a long way to go before we become the people of God You want us to be in our families and as friends. Holy Spirit, we release You within us to be who You say that we are. *We are more than a conqueror in Christ Jesus. We are priests, prophets, and kings. We are fearfully and wonderfully made. We are accepted in the beloved.* Help us to exemplify all of this, especially to our families.

4. You are the lover of our souls. May each family recognize this because of the actions we take daily toward them. Live through us with much patience and grace. Allow this expression to be seen daily. Release the greater understanding of You and Your ways. May this be gained because they see You in us. Give our families and us eyes to see and a heart to realize *the glorious riches of this mystery—You in us...the hope of glory.*

5. We won't be quiet, but continually give You thanks and praise for placing us in the exact right family of Your choosing. We

adore You for a wonderful godly family. We trust You to fashion us into this; therefore, we speak it into existence with this prayer. Even if this has not been the case, we say, "Today is a new day and *nothing is too difficult for our God!"* Even past experiences, bad memories, and sins of all type must bow to the name of Jesus. *We know that You are able to make all grace abound toward us* and give us *sufficiency in all things, resulting in good works.*

6. The friends You've given us are an extension of Your love toward us. We are blessed that You have seen fit to give us <u>just</u> enough—not too many that we would be proud and overwhelmed and not too few that we would be lonely or feel neglected. We appreciate that You are the greatest friend and continue to *stick closer than a brother.* Our eyes are upon You as we look at our friends. We regard ourselves to be fortunate and are very thankful indeed.

7. Lord, we yield ourselves to be a *friend to the friendless* as we follow You and act more like You. That's what You would do, so we pattern our lives after Your example. Your Word tells us that <u>*wounds from a friend can be trusted.*</u> Since our friends are a gift from You, we believe that misunderstandings and injuries allow the *testing of our faith to produce perseverance. This perseverance must finish its work so that we may be mature and complete, not lacking anything.* As we go through life and these wounds bring temporary setbacks, we remember that *weeping is for the night; but joy comes in the morning.*

8. Thank You for all that You allow us to go through. It grows us up *into all things*—in all ways…for the glory and praise of Almighty God. Our ways are not shielded from You; even in pain and suffering, we will praise You. Thank You for continuing *to work all things together for our good* because *we do love You and we are called according to Your purposes.*

9. How awesome are Your ways! How incredible are Your thoughts towards us. *We forget not all Your benefits, because we know You forgive all our sins, heal all our diseases, and even redeem our lives from the pit. Thank You for crowning us with love and compassion, satisfying our desires with good things, and restoring our Youth like the eagles.* We praise You even when we're oppressed, because You are continually *working righteousness and justice* for us.

10. Thank You for providential freedom in this nation. We are free because of the finished work of the cross. Even as our freedoms are disappearing, we know that the blood You shed was not in vain, and the work You've completed inside of us was not futile and cannot be legislated away. *Whom the Son sets free is free indeed.* Thank You for such a great and empirical freedom.

11. Thank You for putting us in a body of believers who aspires to advance the Kingdom of God and allow His perfect work to have His perfect way within them, also. We can't imagine traveling this journey alone, with no help and no commitment from fellow-believers. Even though the Church is not yet perfected, Your Word explains that it is Your exclusive *instrument to speak to powers and principalities.* The Church is still the apple of Your eye and the center of Your attention. *You have made all things beautiful in Your time.* Help us to be a worthy representative and ambassador of peace for You. Allow us to function in a way that continually pleases our heavenly Daddy. Do not allow the enemy to sidetrack us or take us numerous times around the same mountain.

12. We yield ourselves to You and say that as much as depends on us, we will live at peace with all to the best of our abilities. Exonerate us when we get off track and don't exemplify peace to all. Forgive us for not thinking as highly of the Church as You do. Pardon us when we fail to pray and give You thanksgiving for the Church, its people, and especially the leadership. So today, we shout, scream, sing, state, declare, decree, and proclaim thanksgiving to You for our families, friends, freedom, and faith! We especially adore You for the body of Christ—Your Church, Your beloved Bride. We declare for the entire world to hear that You are the head of the Church and are worthy of all praise, honor, adoration, and thanksgiving….in Jesus' name we pray, Amen!

Prayer Twenty Six:
The Prayer of the Bride to
our Heavenly Groom

1. Let the praises of God resound forth from our mouths that all might hear and know that You are alive and well, living in the hearts of Your people. Your presence is what we long for. Your presence is the desire that wells within us. The thought of You overwhelms us wherever we are and causes us to transcend this world into the next while we're technically still seated on earth.

2. How is that possible? How does it happen? Only You know. Yet, You are the one who draws us into that place. You are the one who overshadows everything else so that in all things, we choose You! How that delight takes us higher and higher. We yield ourselves once again. We are sold-out, love-sick children who must be with our Maker.

3. Who can understand this? Only those who have been drawn into the secret place of Your presence or those who long to go there and be with You can even begin to grasp this. One minute we think we understand; the next we can't even begin to wrap our minds around something too wonderful for words. This is not an illusion of our imaginations. So, we wait on You. We revel in this fact. *You are God and there is none like You.* The King of Kings is the lover of our souls.

4. You are the Bridegroom and as a part of Your church, we are Your Bride. We relish in this fact and try to grasp what that really means. Yet, the words are evasive and we are unable to articulate a feeling, a thought, a sensation, a devotion, or a delight— something so indescribable, yet so real. This mystery eludes us, and yet Your presence is tangible. We can feel it, touch it, smell it, and breathe it. Is this really possible? We say "YES!" The King of the universe draws us away just to be with Him—no distractions—nothing impeding a holy visitation.

5. This is our cry: "We have to have more of You. We are not satisfied with yesterday's portion. We have to have more for today. Let the newness of each day's dawning bring forth the freshness of Your presence." Even as freshly baked bread comes from the oven and offers the aroma, taste, texture, and delight that is available only when it first comes from the oven, so we

long for the *Bread of Life* to refresh us anew every day. We long for Your presence to transcend every aspect of our lives.

6. Do not let one area go untouched. We yield all to You! Whatever pleases You is what our hearts are set on. Whatever is on Your heart is what ours beats for. Overflow us; flood us with the realness of LIFE that comes from a living God. There is so much more. Teach us and train us to tap into the **more**.

7. Allow there to be no regrets when our days come to an end. We choose to know You TODAY so that when we take the step from this world into the next, it is as natural as breathing. When we come face to face with the One whom our hearts long for, there is no holding back—no shyness but only the revelation that we have spent our entire life on that which is truly worth it. We want to know You in the **now**. We want to fellowship with You on an intimate and personal level.

8. That is our prayer and our cry. "We will not hold back; we will only go forward." In the process, we release ourselves, our families, our churches, this area, and this nation to this same knowledge of You. Then, none shall be able to resist the calling and grace of God on their lives. Because of this, *the mountains and hills* will no longer need *to cry out*, for the people of God will take their rightful places and release this marvelous act of worship.

9. Lord, turn our entire lives into an act of worshipping You, our King. We cannot do it without Your transforming help; You have all that we need to make it happen. Let our actions be a mirror image of what You are doing and saying in Heaven. Allow us to be vessels that You flow through to bring this to earth. Give us the tenacity to walk this out with grace from on high.

10. Help holiness and purity pour forth from us like the morning dew covering the earth. Allow nothing You have for us to escape to naught and become a tool used against us by the enemy. Help us not to feign accomplishing Your will in the earth today. It is for this time and purpose that we have been born; we even yield that to You. May the days we were born be sweetness to Heaven's calendar as we participate as part of the Esther generation.

11. Help us accomplish what we were created for. Let nothing escape and dissipate as vapor. Allow all we do to return once again and water the ground of the seeds You've planted through us in the fertile soil of Your presence. We yearn to produce a

rich harvest that the King of Kings and Lord of Lords would take pleasure in. We yield even that to You and Your ways. Let the infinite wisdom of our Lord be a *jewel in our crowns that we toss at Your feet* at the right moment. We want to know that we've done what we were created to do, holding nothing back, continually flowing in God's holy stream, gaining momentum in the river of God until Your perfect will is done on earth as it is in Heaven and You receive the glory due Your precious name—Jesus. In Your name we pray, Amen!

Prayer Twenty Seven:
Releasing the Mind and the Five Senses to Pray, Study, Listen, and Wait

1. Who can know the mind of Christ? These great and factual revelations are available for all to partake. It is for the learned and unlearned, the teacher and the student. God makes it freely available to all who would study, pray, wait, and listen. Our prayer today is simply, "Give us a heart to study, to pray, to wait, and to listen. Give us the ability that takes us past the path of least resistance to the place of pressing and self-control."

2. Today we look to the Holy Spirit, the third person of the Trinity, and cry out for guidance and grace. We have to go beyond scratching the surface. We're desperate to go to the deeper depths and to the higher heights. Our goal is to know the delights of Your heart, our God and King. Our choice is to find the threads of revelation and knowledge that are found in diligently searching the Word *to see if these things be so.*

3. Our heart is to go past the basics and foundational to the deeper dwellings of water that are pure, clean, and undefiled. We push past and know that we can go there. So, we lay down the things that hinder us…sin which is obvious. But, we also lay down fears and trepidations that keep us closed off from a reality that can only be entered into by faith and giving of ourselves and time. We yield all of that. We lay it down. We give it up. We press past us to find YOU!

4. We settle on this: there is more, and we want it. We release all of our senses to be anointed by the Holy Spirit. For our eyes, we receive spiritual salve that releases us to the place where Jesus saw what His Father was doing and did it. We release our ears to the cleansing oil that will sustain hearing Your voice and moving on it quickly with whole-hearted obedience.

5. We release even our tongues. Let the *coal from Your altar* have its perfect cleansing work that we may walk in a maturity we've never known, seen, or experienced. Let Your breath blow through us that our nostrils are able to receive supernatural smell that communicates into the natural what You are doing in the heavenly realm. May it go back and forth, back and forth…

Your breath breathing through us so that we release heavenly prayers on earth that capture Your attention because they are sweet smells to Your nostrils.

6. Our hands are yielded also. Let the healing glory and heavenly anointing flow through our hands so that the world can truly know that *these signs will accompany those who believe: In Your name we will drive out demons; we will speak in new tongues; we will pick up snakes with our hands; and if we drink deadly poison, it will not hurt us at all; we will place our hands on sick people, and they will get well.*

7. We want more than anything else for You to receive *all the glory and honor and power* that is due Your name. We want **people everywhere** to stand up and take notice of the kingship of the Kings of Kings and Lord of Lords. To realize this even in our own lives, we also yield to You our mind. We release it to be in alignment with Your thoughts and ways. We release it to think, dwell, ponder, meditate, wonder, contemplate, and reflect upon You, Your words, and Your ways.

8. We release ourselves for Your glory and purposes. We get serious about *thinking on whatever is true, whatever is noble, whatever is right, whatever is pure, whatever is lovely, whatever is admirable—if anything is excellent or praiseworthy,* we choose freely now to exercise self-control and force our minds to only contemplate these things. We want to contemplate *whatever we have learned or received or heard from the Lord, or seen in Him...* we decide, with the help of the Holy Spirit to *put it into practice.* Then and only then, *the God of peace will be with us.*

9. Today, we release this prayer into the atmosphere: "We won't back down from intimately knowing all we can know because we have dwelled with the Most High. We are no longer intimidated by the world, the flesh, or the devil. We have and continue to visit places You alone can take us. We have and will recite words that are too wonderful for our minds to think or imagine. These words **will** flow from the throne room and come out of our mouths. We declare that we **will** speak them and have greater understanding because they are spoken. Power **will** precipitate from them and as we participate with You, more and more is given to us."

10. This continues because we choose to give away all You give us to this lost and dying generation—those on Your heart. So, it's at Your bidding that we speak, prophesy, pray, heal, teach, and touch. We don't take it lightly...but we do freely give it. We offer it to all You direct us to. We have something to give away because **we've made** studying, praying, listening, and waiting a discipline.

11. This metamorphosis continues on an ongoing basis. This discipline becomes our delight. All day long, we yield ourselves to become all that You have created us to be. We teach others to do the same. We see the shift taking place. Our families, churches, areas, and nations are changing—one person, one heart at a time. What's more, the Lover of our souls continues to beckon us because He's in love with us and we bring Him delight. Wow! The impossible becomes possible. Over and over and over again, we come to Your household to receive what we need for our families, friends, and this nation. Thank You for freely giving to us in Jesus' name, Amen!

Prayer Twenty Eight:
Every Day, a Holy Holiday

1. Lord, our delight is in You to do Your bidding and Your will. Allow every day to be a holy holiday in our hearts—like Christmas, Thanksgiving, and Easter. May we worship You continually, choosing to adore You with our lives. May there be no visible heart change in our passion toward You. We choose to live every day for You, with every breath we breathe and all that we are.

2. May the folly of our ways be forgiven and our hearts captured once again by what really matters to You. We shed ourselves of things that displease You, adorning ourselves with the essence of all that You are, that this earth might get a whiff of the fragrance of Your presence. There is none besides You. How we long to worship and adore You in the beauty of holiness. May righteousness and justice beautify our every thought and action. May the God of the universe look and know pleasure because his children have followed him with holy abandonment.

3. Lord, it is You whom we seek and long for. It is You whom we trust with everything. The inward places of our hearts that are hidden from all but You choose to adore the risen King, even as we would on Resurrection Sunday. Our thoughts are brand new every day, like the dawning of the day or the birth of King Jesus. The brightness of Your presence enhances everything about us and causes others to follow, even as the shepherd and the Magi sought their King.

4. Every moment of every day we choose to walk in Thanksgiving. We do thank and praise You from the inside out with all that we are. We shout it over and over, "We choose You! We choose You! We choose You!" It may sound ridiculous to others. We don't care! We repent for not celebrating You every day in our hearts. We repent for not allowing the preeminence of Your kingship to come forth every single day of our lives.

5. Yes! We choose to be merry all the time. We choose to rejoice in our Abba, Father, Daddy every moment. We choose to be thankful always! We admit that we haven't done this, and for that we are sorrowful—with a godly sorrow that leads to true

repentance. We have been created in Your image. We choose to be celebratory every day. We will not be distracted by times or a season, as the world declares it.

6. We speak to our hearts and tell them to align. At the same time, we choose to live each day celebrating the Lordship of the Godhead like it is at Christmas, Easter, or Thanksgiving. In all things, to the best of our abilities, we choose to be grateful. We speak to our souls and command them to line up with Your Word. It will not allow the pantheon of voices to assign its value.

7. It will align itself with the one true God and all Your ways. As revelation comes and truth is disclosed, we will throw off those ideas, opinions, and values that we once felt to be important but do not align with You and Your heart values. We are alive to honor You every day with our lives and the way that we live.

8. So we set our faces like flint to live in a way that brings respect, glory and honor day in and day out to the King of Kings and Lord of Lords. Your will and life are reflected in all that we do and in every kindness we show. May You shine Your presence through us that the hearts and minds of all who meet us encounter You. The result is lovesick people who are *ruined* forever. You have stolen our hearts. It is reserved for no other lover. The deepest recesses are set aside for You. None can pluck You from us.

9. The mystery continues…on and on! What does this look like? What does this sound like? What does this feel like? Since You are new every day, so are the sights, sounds, and feelings that we encounter. Our unchanging God changes not—yet You are always showing us a new facet of Your character and presence. How we love to adorn ourselves with You. We give You all thanks, honor and praise in Jesus' holy and precious name! Amen!

Prayer Twenty Nine:
Prayer for Israel

1. The dregs of our souls wait for You. We allow the transforming presence of Your ways to overtake and overcome us. We yield even the dark unknown areas to You. We drink in the peace that comes as a result of waiting. Teach us to wait. Allow the strength that comes from this discipline to enhance every area of our lives and being.
2. Allow our thoughts to be transformed because we have sought You above all else. The pleasure of this is like a delightful aroma. It rises all about us. It is more powerful than an aphrodisiac or any of the pleasures the world has to offer. Your transforming presence awakens us and allows us to be who You created us to be and not what we try hopelessly to attain.
3. In this yielding we find ourselves made brand new, changed in so many ways that can only be done with the touch of the Master's hands. It is like the stroke of a brush on the painting of our lives—only You can do it. So, we release ourselves to Your will and Your Kingship. We allow You to establish us fully.
4. Help us to be more yielded and not hold back but to give all that You expect from Your children. Focus us so that we do not get sidetracked or continue around the same mountain over and over, never quite allowing You to be as real in us as You want to be. We declare today that it is time for us to stop playing and engage in the godly pursuit that we were created to enjoy and destined to participate in. We release this continually; it echoes between Heaven and earth. We decree, "Let Your presence, anointing, and glory go forth and do the work that You intend it to do." Hear our hopeful, faith-filled cry today!
5. We choose willingly to forsake the former things in order to take on Your new ways! Lord, establish a nation of people who have the same thoughts, prayers, and actions that align with You and Your Word. Begin with us! Help us and all who claim **You** as their Savior to rightly divide Your Word, so that we know what is on Your heart and mind. Help the Church become exercised to hear Your voice and know the difference between what is real and what is counterfeit.

6. We declare, "Arise godly leaders and don't back down or shrink in the face of adversity or calamity!" We cry out for the appointment of true leaders—apostles, prophets, pastors, teachers, evangelists, and lay men and women—who will speak truth and be men and women of courage with their feet firmly established on Your Word, *instant in season and out*, unyielding in the face of wickedness and Biblical compromise.

7. Give us anointing and grace to stop the cycles of wandering that take us away from Your purposes. We set our faces like flint, refusing to travel the same path that produces the same results that leads to hypocrisy and lukewarm living. We cry out also for our families and churches. Help none hold onto the old ways. We willingly, to the best of our ability, forsake former things that are no longer Your agenda. At the same time, we refuse to abandon our foundational values which are established to shepherd the new waves of Your anointing and presence.

8. Help us leave behind the sinfulness of selfishness and focus on ushering in Your second coming. Lord, allow this nation to be set apart to You and You alone. Let us not turn our backs on the spiritual roots and heritage that were established by our forefathers. Help us not to disown our spiritual legacy and the resultant presence that nations established under You enjoy. Allow leaders to understand this and never depart from Your ways. Forgive us for tolerance that leads to unholy mixture.

9. Forgive us for turning our back on Israel, especially since we know that those who bless Israel will in turn be blessed. Allow this nation to view Israel as You view her. Help us, Lord. It is a time that the seriousness of the days in which we live be considered and examined carefully. Once again our cry is for **help** in this nation, over this area, in churches, and families." This is a critical time in the history of man. Do not let it be said that we failed to *fast, pray, seek Your face, and turn from our wickedness.*

10. Teach us to love the sinner while forsaking and hating the sin. Allow Your presence to capture hearts and minds; cause the unregenerate and those who are lukewarm to turn to You and repent. Orchestrate this in such a way *that hearts melt like wax* as Your plans and strategies come forth for individuals, families, churches, and nations. Help us to not get caught up in the latest and greatest or most popular Christian wave to distract us from

the very heart and will of what You are really saying and doing.

11. Don't allow our so-called *freedoms* to be a stumbling block to those who are hurting and in pain. Lord, help us to forsake our will in the name of love and for the sake of Your Gospel. Help us to differentiate between the two and view everything with the mind of Christ—from Your perspective. Father, forgive us when we've not done this...when the hardness of our hearts has separated us from You and Your people.

12. Pursue us, Lord, with a passion that will cause us never to resist You. We need You <u>now</u> more than ever. Our hearts are pliable. Mold them to Your ways that will impact this dying and lost generation. Even now, we yield to You all that we are or ever will be. Use us to advance Your Kingdom on earth. That is our cry, in Jesus' name, Amen!

Prayer Thirty:
Perfecting the Saints

1. Lord, let Your light so shine in us and through us that others will see and give glory, honor, and praise to You—*the One who is, who was, who is to come.* There is none like You—none grander or greater than You, my Lord. Let the fragrance of Your presence in us arise. Allow us to drink in the pleasures of our King so that the results may be felt by those with whom we come in contact.

2. We cry out, "Let all the people of God, including us, arise to the newness of this day and participate in the things that are on the Father's heart." We decree, "That which we hear and see will remain in the center of our hearts and at the forefront of our minds. Do not allow even a minuscule part to escape from our thoughts, actions, or deeds."

3. Forsaking not the former things You taught us, we step into that which is new—the NOW season in the Spirit. We hearken [listen and pay attention] to realize what is on Your heart and walk in it. Even when the seasons change, we release ourselves to choose the new ways. We give up that which was comfortable and familiar.

4. Lord, we long for You in this NOW time and season. We long for the freshness of the day. We want to be on the cutting edge of what You're doing. Will You take us to that place? Will You hold our hands and guide us there? We are longing for more of You and reaching upward to receive it.

5. We don't delight that our flesh feels tension in this, wars against us, and sometimes yearns for the *good ole days.* That one fact keeps us on our knees, pressing...pressing...pressing...and evermore repenting. In the midst of this, we have learned to trust You and submit ourselves to Your good will and pleasure.

6. It is for Your name's sake that we journey *the less traveled road.* It is for the advancement of Your Kingdom that we command ourselves—body, soul, and spirit—to line up with You and Scripture. Our goal is to be so recklessly abandoned that we do not take our eyes from You—*the prize,* not even for a moment.

7. Even if the way seems treacherous and full of danger, we behave like *good soldiers,* obeying our commander-in-chief, Jesus. *We press on* proclaiming truth. You are trustworthy and will *never leave us nor forsake us.* You will only do those things that are in keeping *with the perfecting of the saints. That good and perfect work You began in us will be completed. Here we are, Lord. M*old us!"

8. Sometimes our finite minds are overwhelmed by the greatness of an infinite God. As we ponder upon things You've placed in us that are too marvelous for words, we question whether the folly of our prayers will get us in trouble. Lord, we don't want to pray prayers that are *meaningless.* Ecclesiastes states...*everything is meaningless.* We trust You and choose to live our lives just the opposite because Your peace surrounds us and You order our footsteps! So we refuse to be swayed and journey onward, covering ourselves with this declaration, *"Your will be done—not ours."*

9. Lord, give us optimism that we would not grow weary. Sanction our hearts to absorb only things that are important to You. We tune our spiritual antenna to pick up Your signals, sound waves, and impulses only. We declare freedom from the trickery of the enemy over us, our families, our churches, and this area.

10. Allow us to set our eyes on truth in the midst of 'jibber-jabber' from others and the media that is all around us. Give us the correct focus that absorbs heavenly values and spiritual insights. May we never grow so weary that we give up the fight! Help us be one of many who take a stand and hold on, even when it appears that others are caving in to political correctness and worldliness.

11. May we never give up on the fact that You are a God who loves every person individually and You are able to *work all things together for* our *good* and Your glory. We also choose to remember *that You are interceding for us at the right hand of the Father.* Your prayers assure us that *our faith will not fail.* Thank You for praying prayers before we even know our needs. We exclaim to all, "How great is our God!"

12. Lord, let Your people stand and rejoice in You and You alone. As You are an advocate for justice, we surrender to that, also. May Your love spill over to us and through us for the helpless and hurting, that they might obtain justice, also. Allow us to be

more pro-life than we've ever been—not just talking the talk, but walking the walk. Permit these prayers to go forth to *stop abortion and release LIFE.*

13. There is no glory inherently in us, but we are a reflection of You—a vessel and a conduit on this earth. Allow Your power to flow through us mightily. Allow us *to hide Your Word in our hearts*; help us *to rightly divide it.* Don't permit our flesh to dictate our future. Assist us in continuing Your path of righteousness and holiness. We hold on to the fact that You are our *all in all.* You alone are the one who is worthy of all preeminence and glory. So, today we dedicate ourselves to You—with all our actions, thoughts, and deeds. Receive it as a sacrifice that we offer to You, our Lord and King. In Jesus' name, we praise You for all this—a complete work, Amen!